'Prepare to be shocked, rocked and mocked in this g̶ laugh-out-loud-funny, lovingly crafted, meticulously researched, spookily insightful and accurately spelled guide to all things thespian. Since reading it, my approach to auditioning, rehearsing and surviving in the West End has dramatically improved.'
Michael Ball

'Don't even consider putting your daughter on the stage, Mrs Worthington, until you've first consulted this wonderful book.'
Paul O'Grady

'A deliciously wicked eavesdrop into the side of the business that is kept under wraps. Uber-hilarious and unputdownable.'
Frances Barber

'Scabrous, scurrilous, hilarious and at the same time informative, perceptive and essential reading for the professional and enthusiast alike. Irresistible.' **Colin Baker**

'Highly amusing, brilliantly blunt, surprisingly informative... Everything you *really* need to know about theatre.'
Bonnie 'Three Kills' Langford

'In an industry where 99% of your time is spent working out the difference between what is being said and what is actually meant (the other 1% being spent removing pubic hair from between your teeth), it seems that one man – a man of integrity, experience and with nothing to hide – has penned a definitive translation. He handed me my copy with the words, "What you hold in your hand now could well be the making of you." And although not the first producer to have uttered those words to me, he was the first to say them whilst I was holding a book.' **Rufus Hound**

'Toss off your Stanislavsky, your Meisner and your Strasberg. Slip this into your doublet and hose; it's all you need to know about this business called show.' **Brendan Coyle**

'To be able to walk, talk and act all at the same time is something I could only dream of. West End Producer has shown me that dreams really can come true.' **Jill Halfpenny**

'If you can stop yourself from laughing at the many wise and pin-point observations about this crazy business, you will actually find some genuinely good advice for a career in the theatre. Whether you're a beginner or an old ham like me, there is much to amuse and enlighten.' **David Harewood**

'West End Producer is the Invisible Man of Theatreland. Whether savagely sloshed or nursing hangovers at auditions, his insights are always wickedly funny.' **Reece Shearsmith**

'West End Producer is the naughty little man who dares to tell the truth. If you want to learn about the real life of an actor, this book is for you.' **Melanie C**

'Outspoken, biting, merciless... and I absolutely love it!' **Ruthie Henshall**

'West End Producer is the naughtiest man in theatre. What he doesn't know about acting isn't worth knowing.' **Stephen Mear**

'Hilariously honest. It made me cry with laughter!' **Andy Nyman**

'West End Producer has caught the eyes of the whole West End Twitter world. Now *that's* talent.' **Kerry Ellis**

'The jazz-hands master of showbiz tweets.' **Susan Penhaligon**

'West End Producer's words of wisdom have taught me how to walk, talk and act all at the same time.' **Al Murray**

'Without West End Producer I'd never have discovered the "squint your eyes and look intense" look. A crucial part of my performance now.' **Louise Dearman**

'Everything I know about acting I learnt from this book... and a pissed tramp living in the car park under the National Theatre.' **Con O'Neill**

'West End Producer is a fountain of theatrical knowledge. If you want honest, brilliant advice about the business, he's your man, dear!' **Aled Jones**

'West End Producer taught me that the casting couch is the only way to get a job.' **Ian 'H' Watkins**

WEST END PRODUCER

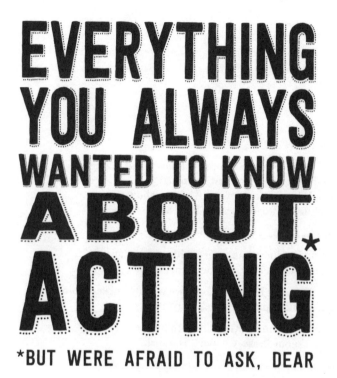

EVERYTHING YOU ALWAYS WANTED TO KNOW ABOUT* ACTING

*BUT WERE AFRAID TO ASK, DEAR

NICK HERN BOOKS
London
www.nickhernbooks.co.uk

A NICK HERN BOOK

*Everything You Always Wanted to Know About Acting**
first published in Great Britain in 2013
by Nick Hern Books Limited, The Glasshouse,
49a Goldhawk Road, London W12 8QP

Copyright © 2013 West End Producer

West End Producer has asserted his moral right
to be identified as the author of this work

Author photo by Matt Crockett (www.mattcrockett.com)
Designed and typeset by Nick Hern Books

Printed and bound in Great Britain by
Ashford Colour Press, Gosport, Hampshire

A CIP catalogue record for this book is available
from the British Library

ISBN 978 1 84842 347 3

MIX
Paper from
responsible sources
FSC
www.fsc.org   FSC® C011748

* *But Were Afraid to Ask, Dear*

For

*My Jean Valjean teddy – who is there for me every night,
ensuring I am never 'On My Own'*

and

*My dear family – who are a constant source of inspiration,
surprise, and unending support*

Contents

Acting is problem-solving. Directing is helping with the problem. And producing is paying to make the problem look good, dear.

Acknowledgements

Firstly, I would like to thank everyone who has supported me whilst working on this book. I have a tendency to get very moody after long hours staring at my laptop – so I must send sincere love and thanks to my loving and understanding partner. Thank you for going through this journey with me.

I must also thank everyone who has helped keep the mystery of WEP still a secret! There are times when the temptation to 'out me' must be excruciating, so I sincerely thank you for your kind support, humour, and constant help in making this possible. To my dear friends who have given up so much of their time to help, assist and advise – I cannot thank you enough. You know who you are...

To my wonderful Twitter followers and family – people who have become dear friends and colleagues as a result of the internet. To the 'angels' who firstly took an interest in my work, and to everyone else who has come along and enjoyed the fun. To Anne, Susan, Lynne, Linda, Gemma, Dompy, Mike, Robert, Rebecca, Janie, Julian, Steve, Adam – and especially Trevor, who has been a constant guide – thank you.

To Michael and Tony, who have a passion for new talent like myself – thank you for your ongoing enthusiasm.

Humble thanks to all the well-known faces and showbiz friends who have dedicated their time and energy to read my book and let me have their thoughts. You are all living proof that there are 'no people like show people'.

Thanks to my editor, Matt Applewhite at Nick Hern Books, who has made the creation and development of this book such a joy. For your patience, understanding and intelligence, you have my sincere thanks – and Dom to follow! Also everyone else at Nick Hern Books, who are a delight, a joy, and constant source of inspiration – thank you.

And, of course, to my dear parents – without whom none of this would have been possible. With love.

WEP

The Overture

My dears! Welcome to my little book, all about acting, theatre, entertainment, and the business of show. I do hope you enjoy it.

I spend many evenings discussing the theatre, and felt it was about time I wrote all of my thoughts and experiences down. I wanted to write something that reflected how it is to work in theatre and entertainment in the present day. The truth is that the art of acting and showbiz is, sadly, not all glitz, glamour and jazz hands.

A few years ago I was struck with a sense of doom as I worked alongside some people who took their job far too seriously. Acting and entertainment is, of course, a business, and like any business has to be taken seriously. But this business is also about creating joy and entertainment. There is nothing as rewarding as observing a creative company coming together to put on a show. They are a family, a community working towards one shared goal and often for no money. What other profession can make such a claim? And this is what makes theatre so magical: the astonishing combination of energy, enthusiasm and commitment at the heart of everyone working in it.

I hope this book dispels some of the myths and fears about acting, and provides an honest guide to the realities of entertainment in the modern age. There is a lot of fear in the business. People, especially actors, often feel that they can't voice their true opinions because they don't want to get a bad reputation. There are whispers in corridors, murmurs in The Ivy, and speculation in Andrew Lloyd Webber's office, but a lot of what happens in theatre stays in its own little world. I am not attempting to 'dish the dirt' on theatre at all – I just want to open the door a little wider.

As you read this book I suggest taking the time to practise your jazz hands and do the odd ball-change in between chapters. It will give you a great sense of theatre wherever you are. And theatre is the one thing we could all do with more of. So come inside, have a read, take from it what you will, and enjoy, dear.

According to *Fame*, 'Acting is the hardest profession in the world.' Personally, I think brain surgery ranks quite high up there as well, dear.

THE PRE-SHOW: TRAINING

OR
LEARNING HOW TO WALK AND TALK – AT THE SAME TIME

Stanislavsky called. He said forget about his
books – it's all about tits and teeth, dear.

Training

Drama schools are marvellous places. They are filled with eager young performers and talented staff who want to share their wisdom, knowledge and phone numbers. But is it essential for an actor to go to drama school? In my mind, a drama-school training is very important – it provides actors with a solid basis and foundation in all aspects of a performer's life. They teach everything from walking and talking to singing and shouting – and importantly provide you with useful contacts in the professional world. Of course, I am not saying that to be a successful actor you *must* go to drama school – there are many marvellous performers who have never stepped foot in one. But it is just a lot tougher to do it that way. Going to a good drama school implies that you have trained to a high standard and can enter and exit the stage without getting an erection.

Auditioning for drama school is a long and arduous process, and requires years of research and development. There are many things to consider; for example, what kind of actor do you want to become? All drama schools offer different specialised courses – ranging from musical theatre, acting, dancing, and reality TV technique. So you need to decide what kind of an actor you want to be. You will find very early on in your career that you are typecast as a certain type of performer straight away. Which is why I suggest that pole-dancing is not your first professional engagement.

There are many types of drama schools. Whilst some are based in lovely big mansion houses in the middle of acres of land, others can be found near brothels in King's Cross. Of course, this does not mean that one is better than the other – it just means that at one you can expect a more varied and fulfilling personal life. There are currently twenty-one drama schools which belong to Drama UK (formerly the Conference of Drama Schools), and also many others – and the task of deciding which one is right for you can lead to decades of uncertainty, dizziness and celibacy. It is essential you do your research and discover which ones have the best-looking staff, cleanest toilets and cheapest bar. These tiny details will make all the difference in your drama training.

You should also do your research and discover which famous actors and celebrities attended each school. It is always very telling when a school is proud to advertise that they have a recent graduate who is fronting the new Durex advert, or appearing in a nursery school's tour of *Trainspotting*.

Most drama schools have the words 'dramatic', 'art' or 'academy' in their title (some are very greedy and have all three). A few have the word 'Royal' in them – which simply means that Prince Edward goes there at weekends to work on his drag act. Occasionally you will even find a school that has the word 'music' in it. This means that, as well as a couple of hours of drama each week, you also get a few minutes to play the recorder and practise your fingering skills.

Choosing a Drama School

In honesty, if a casting director has two identical CVs in front of them and one actor trained at RADA and one trained at the Louie Spence Academy – the actor who went to RADA would get the job. This rule doesn't apply if the other actor happens to be sleeping with the casting director, or has a famous parent. Famous parents are very useful for both getting into drama school and finding work in the industry. I have heard countless stories of actors refusing to use their parents' names and contacts when starting in the industry. This is a mistake. If your parent is famous then they will have lots of contacts – which will inevitably save you years of waking up next to old, smelly directors.

A few years ago I knew an actor who changed his name so he could pretend to be Judi Dench's son. For some reason everyone presumed he was telling the truth – and as a result he got lots of nice theatre and television work. But eventually someone worked out he wasn't in actual fact her son – and was forced to revert back to his real name: Lenny Henry. Bless him.

It is also important to consider where the drama school is. A drama school in central London is marvellous as it is easy for agents to come and watch you perform. A drama school in Essex is not so handy – unless you are particularly keen to appear on *TOWIE*.

Another factor you have to think about is the expense of living in certain areas. For example, RADA is based near lovely Bloomsbury – so accommodation is very expensive. On the other hand, Mountview is based in Wood Green – which is a much cheaper area to live. Although the chances of getting stabbed there are a lot higher, dear.

....

What is the difference between a one-year and a three-year acting course? About twenty thousand pounds, dear.

....

There is also the question of whether to do a one-year or a three-year course. Both are full-time courses, and offer a thorough practical training in drama. A one-year course is basically a three-year course condensed into a year, and is aimed at older students, people who have already been to university, and people who can already speak without dribbling. In truth, although a one-year course gives a good training, in the business they are not looked on as highly as a three-year course. You will obviously have a showcase at the end of the year, but far fewer agents and casting directors go to them. This is primarily because agents think that someone who has trained for three years will be better as they have far more experience. However, if you can't decide between a one-year and a three-year course, some drama schools offer a two-year course. In my mind, though, the more training you can get, the better. Most drama schools charge around nine thousand pounds a year. And on top of this you also have to pay for maintenance, as drama schools tend not to offer student accommodation. Of course, you may be lucky and get a scholarship or a DaDA (Dance and Drama Award), which will help with tuition and maintenance. And then the only thing you have to worry about is beer money, dear.

....

New acting graduates have a very big advantage over other actors: no reputation.

....

The Drama-school Audition

There are usually two different types of auditions: private/ individual auditions – where you audition on your own for the panel. And group auditions – where a group of audition-ees go in together and perform in front of each other. The panel will always consist of drama-school tutors, successful graduates, and a dinner lady.

These days you have to pay a fee to audition for drama schools. These can vary, but are normally about £50 each. The money made from the auditions goes into a savings account for the staff Christmas party. Some people think this is a naughty waste of school funds – but these people obviously have no idea how expensive Stringfellows is.

Because of the expense involved in auditioning, it is vital you choose wisely when considering which schools to apply for. As well as the expense of the audition itself, you have to consider the additional expense of travelling to and from the audition – which you will have to pay for again if you get a recall. It's all money, money, money before you've even got a place! In truth, auditioning for a drama school is like a full-time job, and with the ever-increasing costs the time will come when potential students will need a grant to just cover their audition expenses.

Once you've applied, paid and been offered an audition, you just need to prepare for the audition itself. One of the most important things to prepare is your hair. As a general rule, RADA favours floppy hair, Mountview favours short hair, and ArtsEd favours no hair (the smoother the better).

You will usually be asked to prepare both Shakespeare and modern monologues. This is where the confusion begins. Many people believe the word 'prepare' simply means reading the speech out loud. It doesn't. 'Preparing your speech' means: reading it, learning it, speaking it, and walking it – *ideally at the same time*. It's also a bonus if you understand what you're talking about (although this is not mandatory).

If you are finding your Shakespeare speech difficult to perform, I suggest working on the 'iambic pentameter'. The iambic pentameter is something that Peter Hall invented one day as a joke, but actors started taking it seriously. Basically you say 'de-dum-de-dum-de-dum-de-dum-de-dum' whenever you don't understand what Shakespeare has written. Many actors use this method, particularly at the RSC. In fact, there was a famous production of *Henry V* starring Kenneth Branagh where he said 'de-dum-de-dum-de-dum-de-dum-de-dum' instead of the actual written lines. It was a roaring success, and in all honesty was the first time I understood what Shakespeare was going on about, dear.

A modern speech doesn't necessarily have to be from a play based on a housing estate in South London about drugs and gang warfare – although this will help. You can also do speeches from modern texts that have recently been performed at the Royal Court, National Theatre and the Bush.

The Bush is a particular favourite of mine for the simple reason that it reminds me of the 'lady garden' area. Modern speeches tend to contain swear words – but if you don't like swearing I suggest substituting them for something more tolerable. Words like 'rabbit', 'sponge' and 'knitting' always go down well.

If you are having difficulty finding a suitable modern speech, I advise the following: a good one will have shouting, crying and a little bit of laughter. It could also involve nudity. Of course, this is not essential – but drama tutors love that sort of thing.

....

Actors – doing a two-day Shakespeare workshop at RADA doesn't mean you trained there.

....

The Musical-theatre Audition

When auditioning for musical-theatre courses you will inevitably be asked to sing a song. I always advise singing a musical-theatre song – although most pieces of modern pop and rock music tend to end up in musicals these days anyway.

When deciding what to sing, certain things need to be considered: make sure you can sing all the notes, make sure you know what the song is about, and make sure it's not from *Les Misérables* or *Miss Saigon*. This is simply because they are overused (and also nice young girls from Surrey don't do French peasants or Vietnamese whores very well). It is also important to sing through the song with a pianist before your actual audition – as the piano accompaniment is always very different from the original soundtrack recording you have been copying.

Whilst we're on the subject of pianists, you should always check that the piano accompaniment isn't too hard. Many pianists who play for drama-school auditions have only just passed their Grade 3 piano exam – so playing Lloyd Webber songs is fine. But you must never give these kinds of pianists sheet music by Stephen Sondheim or Jason Robert Brown. They will invariably give up halfway through and revert back to playing *Starlight Express*.

Many people believe that the higher the song, the more impressive it will be. This simply isn't true. Particularly if you can't sing it! There is no point singing a song that goes up to a top C when you can only sing a top A.

The Chat

At the end of your audition, the panel will have a little chat with you about why you want to go to their school, your past experience, and why you want to be an actor. At this point it is always good to sound intelligent and give the impression that you have done your research. You should state exactly why you want to go to RADA and not Italia Conti (obviously this can be the other way round, depending on where you want to go). It is never recommended that you slag off other schools, but staff members always like to have their school praised. Things like: 'Your school produces the best actors', 'The calibre of drama in this country is largely down to the training that your school provides' and 'Your students are the best-looking' always go down well. Avoid saying things like: 'Your school is close to my boyfriend's house', 'My best mate told me this place is really good' and 'I slept with an actor who trained here.'

This is also the time when someone on the panel will bring up the daunting subject of money – and how you plan to finance yourself. If you are in the fortunate position of being able to pay for the course privately (by yourself, or with help from your family) then make this *very* clear. Drama schools adore students who can fund themselves privately. I am not saying that students who can fund themselves have a higher chance of getting a place at drama school – as that would be unfair. There are just an awful lot more of them that get in, dear.

If you find yourself being offered a place at several drama schools you should only accept one. Drama schools, believe it or not, do talk to each other – and if they get wind that you are denying another student a place by selfishly accepting more than one, you will quickly lose all of your offers, and find yourself at home watching *The Jeremy Kyle Show* for another year.

A Concise Guide to Training

If you cannot afford the time and money to go to drama school, here is a summary of what is taught there:

Audition technique – Be prepared. Be confident. Face the panel. And don't cry.

Stage technique – Know where to enter and exit. Face the audience. Speak loudly. Don't look at the floor.

Acting technique – Say your lines loudly and in order. Look at the other people on stage with interest. Do not gurn or dribble.

Dancing technique – Smile. Use jazz hands frequently. And don't fall over. If you aren't very confident, just stand at the back and jump up and down.

Singing technique – Sing the melody and avoid looking like a blow-up doll.

Actors – the most important thing to learn at drama school is how to sit in a circle, dear.

ACT ONE: AUDITIONING

OR
STANDING, SPEAKING, SINGING, SMILING, SIGHING, SULKING AND SCREAMING

When you audition there's always a moment when you're perfect for the role. It's just before you come through the door.

Auditioning

Auditions are an essential part of being an actor. They are the time when an actor has the opportunity to prove why they are perfect for the job. These days it is virtually impossible to get a job without auditioning, unless you have been on *Celebrity Big Brother*.

The aim of an audition is simple: to go in and be brilliant! You should never compare yourself to other actors you see going in before you – as you never know how good they are. They may be wearing the nicest clothes, be talking about their latest film and gloating about their last West End show – but for all you know they could be pathological liars on day release from their agent's dungeon. Everyone thinks everyone else is better than them. But no one is better than you. You are unique.

Always turn up early for your audition – just so you can question the other actors who are there already. Ask them what they are singing, what the show is about, and if they know who the casting director's boyfriend is. This is all useful ammunition for when you get into the audition room. Also, if you can hear what they are doing in the audition room you can steal their ideas, dear.

Get up, put on your favourite lipstick, your best heels, smile widely, get in that audition room, and kick ass, dear.

The Auditioning Process

Auditioning is not as simple as just turning up in a tank top, wandering into the audition room and belting out 'One Day More' at the top of your lungs. It takes a lot more time, dedication, and planning permission than that.

I often advise young actors to audition for any work at the beginning of their careers, just for the experience. Doing a small-scale tour of Beirut, or a primary-school tour of *Puppetry of the Penis*, for example, would offer you lots of hands-on experience. However, I've heard that some bigger agents don't allow their clients to do any work outside of London. They just want them to hang around bus stops and jazz clubs and wait for big film offers to come flooding in. Invariably when the film offer does come along it tends to be two lines in a feature about a drug-dealing teenager who lives on a council estate in Brixton. So, even then, it's not particularly glamorous, dear.

You will have to prepare yourself for the fact that to get the job you will usually have at least nine unpaid recalls. The simple reason for this is because those of us on the audition panel often forget what all the actors look and sound like. Obviously we try and make notes during auditions – but sometimes we get distracted by thinking about our lunch, particularly if you are singing something by Jason Robert Brown. There's nothing wrong with Jason Robert Brown, but there's only so many times you can listen to 'Still Hurting' without actually hurting someone.

Frequently I get asked why we never give an answer to actors straight after their audition. Whilst I agree it would be very easy for us, and a lot fairer on the actors – we generally make them wait for days, weeks, and sometimes months. There is no real reason for this, apart from the fact that sometimes we get distracted by reruns of *The West Wing*.

Actors sometimes get angry when we don't call their agents to let them know they didn't get the job. Please understand that this is not done on purpose, and if I had my way all actors would get a telephone call telling them 'yes' or 'no'. The only reason this doesn't happen is because my casting director gets confused about who actually got the job and who didn't (as everyone looks so similar) – so it's safer if he doesn't call anyone. Also, if my casting director had to call everyone he auditioned he wouldn't be able to get on with more important things, like plumping the cushions on his casting couch, dear.

Of course, there are valid reasons why we sometimes keep actors waiting for long periods – mostly it's because you could be the second or third choice, and we are still waiting for our first choice to give us an answer. We have to keep actors 'on hold' in case the actor we really want decides to turn us down – so that we are sure we have someone who is able to play the role. This is what my casting director means when he tells your agent that you are still 'in the mix'. It means that you are not the first choice, but you may still get the job if everyone else turns us down.

Sadly the sheer number of actors out there makes it impossible for us to audition everyone. Sometimes we will have over two thousand applications for one role – and we just don't have the time to see every actor. So, as a general rule, my casting director goes onto Spotlight, finds the actors with good agents, the actors he fancies, and the actors who have been on telly – and invites those ones in to audition.

The first audition is usually the quickest – as at this stage we are whittling people down, and often don't know what we are looking for. For this audition you will normally be asked to prepare two songs from a specific genre. Examples of these different genres and styles of songs are: upbeat pop, rock ballad, classical aria, modern musical theatre, traditional musical theatre, rock with a hint of pop and rap from a modern musical, traditional musical theatre sung in a Liverpudlian accent, a song from an American songbook musical that is comic and has the word 'cottage' in it, an English patter song that includes a cow impression and is based on a show about a boat – the list goes on. Obviously, even if we don't ask you to sing a specific song, you should still try and choose one that is suitable. We recently had an actor sing 'I'm Just a Girl Who Can't Say No' in his *Oliver!* audition. His agent had obviously not told him he was auditioning for Bill Sikes, dear.

If we like you and think you could possibly play the part, we will give you a recall. You will then be sent some script and music from the show to prepare – usually about six songs and six scenes. Of course, we expect you to learn this material, even if we only send it to you the day before. I recently had an argument with an actor about the amount of material we sent over for him to learn in a day – and after two minutes of listening to him warble on, I reminded him that if he didn't want to do it, someone else will. In the end, John Barrowman agreed and just got on with it.

It is very important that you don't brag to your colleagues and friends when you get a recall. There is nothing worse. It makes you look like an arrogant pig. A recall is just a recall. Don't flatter yourself. There are many reasons we give recalls. Mostly it is because we think you show promise. But sometimes it is simply because we couldn't see your tattoo properly and want to have another look. I know one casting director who always gives recalls to girls who are over six foot purely because he loves tall women. This was never a problem until he cast *Snow White and the Seven Dwarfs*, and all the dwarfs ended up being female giants.

After your first recall there can be lots of other stages. Many of the bigger musicals can take months to cast, and you must anticipate having up to twenty-five recalls before getting an answer. That is when it gets frustrating for actors – as by that stage you feel you've got a pretty good chance of getting the job. But mostly the number of auditions means nothing at all.

Recently there was a show being cast by a very well-known casting director that started auditions two months before the director was available. When the director finally decided to come along at the seventh round of auditions, he told the casting director that they had been looking for the wrong 'types'. This, as you can imagine, was very frustrating for both the actors and casting director. So the casting director had to start the whole process again. And then the director and choreographer got more involved with the auditions – and starting using them to 'workshop' the show. For example, the choreographer tried different dance routines with the auditionees to see what worked. It is a way of working on a show without having to pay any of the actors. And it is wrong. But, of course, actors will do exactly what they're told. So not only were hundreds of actors being tried out and asked to learn and work on dance routines – they were providing a free workshop session for the creative team. However, after nine months, four deaths, a lot of chocolate, and a divorce, the show was finally cast. And the Lewisham schools' tour of *Cinderella* was a huge success.

....

Actors – the use of the word 'amazeballs' in your audition is banned. If I hear it you will be sentenced to a year-long TIE tour, dear.

....

The Different Stages of Auditions

The **1st** audition is the Audition.

The **2nd** audition is the Recall.

The **3rd** audition is the Let's See If They Can Say Dialogue Without Spitting.

The **4th** audition is the Parade Them in a Tight Top in Front of the Director.

The **5th** audition is the Movement Call.

The **6th** audition is the Get Them Back In and See What They Look Like Standing Next to the Lead.

The **7th** audition is the We've Got the Audition Room Booked for Another Day So Let's Call Them Back for a Laugh.

The **8th** audition is the Let's See Who They Can Understudy.

The **9th** audition is the Meet the Producer.

The **10th** audition is the Do They Look Right?

And the **11th** audition is the Can They Actually Do the Job?

Of course, the above is just a general guide to the plethora of auditions that you can be expected to go through. But obviously it's a different story entirely if you're auditioning for the producer Bill Kenwright. For his shows you will have two auditions – one in front of his casting director, and a second in front of the man himself. Then you'll be offered the job and start rehearsing. And the following day you'll be performing in the show. His productions are the fast food of the theatre world. And, just like McDonald's, they look nice under the lights but can leave a bitter taste in your mouth, dear.

If you are unfortunate enough to do eleven auditions and then not get offered the job, you just have to take it with a pinch of salt. As long as you've auditioned to the best of your ability you should be happy, and just accept that something better is waiting around the corner. However, if you are feeling particularly upset about not getting the job it can be quite therapeutic to find out who did and start spreading rumours about their personal hygiene.

Sometimes, after a particularly bad audition, I have seen actors attempt to get a 'sympathy' recall. These are when an actor plucks at the audition panel's heart strings, and tells them something incredibly upsetting – just like those *X Factor* contestants who go through to the next stage simply because their nan recently died. I don't agree with sympathy recalls – but I know some casting directors who love a good sob story.

I have been forced to endure many such stories recently, but only once did it bring my casting director and me to tears. This particular story was about a little cat getting run over. The actress in question told her story after singing the most awful version of 'Defying Gravity' I have ever heard. In truth, it defied gravity that her head didn't explode as she screeched through the final chorus. But she told her cat story with such emotion and pain that we felt guilty and gave her a sympathy recall. Obviously she didn't get the final job, but at least her cat didn't die in vain.

However, if your plight for a sympathy recall doesn't work, you can always just beg. You'd be surprised at the amount of well-known actors who resort to this technique and finish auditions on their knees in front of my casting director.

....

Actors – drinking two cans of Red Bull before an audition does not make you a better actor. It just makes you a shakier one.

....

Auditioning – From My Side of the Table

The casting process is a long, arduous and exhausting business, particularly for the people doing the casting! I equate it to building a rocket out of chocolate – it's hard to do, but when completed is very tasty. Casting directors and directors feel immense pressure to make sure they find the right actors for the job, and in some cases feel just as nervous as the people they are auditioning. So how do we go about casting a show?

One of the most important things we have to remember is what show we are casting. It's no good casting *Othello* if the show is actually *Annie*. This is a vital thing to remember, and one which I often have to remind my casting director about. I knew a director in the eighties who once assembled a fine cast of young actors, only to realise that he actually needed dancers as he was casting a ballet. What a silly prat.

So, after we've decided on the show, we have a few other decisions to make before the casting begins – we have to book a venue, book a lighting designer, have a set designed, assemble a front-of-house team, taste the ice-cream flavours, market the show, drink some Dom, go on a team-building weekend, read Craig Revel Horwood's autobiography, and meditate. Basically we do everything we can to put off the chore of casting until Equity get in touch, slap our wrists and threaten to take our diaries off us unless we start. So, apprehensively, we do.

The next step is in the hands of the casting director. Casting directors are usually very nice people who like drinking far too much alcohol, and mostly during the day. The ones that don't drink usually have other habits, which can't be discussed here – but often end in them being discovered on a bench outside Waterloo Station at 5 a.m.

The first thing the casting director does is to release a 'breakdown'. This doesn't mean he sends out photos of himself in tears, screaming in despair, and taking Prozac. It means he sends out an email of what roles are available. This is usually done through the Spotlight Link – and sent to most agents. Sometimes certain agents will be kept off the list, but only in extreme cases (if they haven't bought me gifts for a long time).

For those that don't know, the Spotlight Link is an online service that allows casting directors to email all agents about castings, and receive submissions in response. It is also widely used by actors who have managed to steal a casting director's password – who use it to stalk and stare at other actors' CVs.

Due to increasing levels of obesity, Spotlight are going to include a 'man boobs' option in their physical-appearance section.

Once the breakdown has been received, your agent will decide which of their clients are right for the part. This involves reading the breakdown – which can be tricky for illiterate agents (an alarmingly high number of them). Luckily these agents are very clever and have assistants or interns. These assistants only have one role: to read out loud to the agents. This avoids embarrassment, and proves invaluable experience.

When the agent has digested the information they will spend a few hours drinking tea, coffee or gin. Then suddenly they'll get inspired and mix some vodka with Red Bull – and away they go! They look at photos of all their clients, and remind themselves whom they represent. Some people think it's easy being an agent, but sometimes they have over twenty actors' names to remember (and sometimes they have an Equity name *and* a real name, which confuses things even more). Once they've reminded themselves of their clients, the agents make honest, considered and well-informed decisions about which actors to put forward to the casting director. Things they must consider are: Do they look right? Are they the right age? Can they do the accent? Can they walk in a straight line? Can they speak loudly? Can they tie their shoelaces? It is tough. And sometimes an agent gets incredibly upset and doesn't know what to do – so decides by using the 'Eeny meeny miny moe, pick an actor for the show' technique.

Once this important decision is made, the casting director will receive an influx of actors suitable for the role. It is not unusual for a casting director to receive more than a thousand suggestions for one role: a huge amount. So the casting director then has to sift through all the submissions and decide which actors to invite for an audition. This is where it gets difficult. Do they bring in new actors who are unknown to them? Do they bring in actors they have employed before? Or do they bring in actors they fancy? Invariably it'll be a mix of all three, with emphasis on the latter.

Then your agent is called and you get offered an audition. You are told an audition time, what to prepare, what role you are up for, and, if you are lucky, the venue for the audition. And then it's all down to you.

....

Actors – when reading to your children at night, always imagine you are auditioning for them. They could grow up to be casting directors, dear.

....

Getting Your Own Auditions

What if you don't get an audition through your agent? Or worse still – what if you don't have an agent? What to do? Well, when this happens you usually have two options. One: admit defeat. Two: get in contact yourself. Some agents are not fans of their clients trying to get an audition themselves, but it has worked in the past for actors I know. You just have to be very professional in the way you do it. One email, or letter, clearly stating what part you are interested in, is enough. If you want to include gift vouchers, expensive organic chocolates or Dom – then this helps. However, never pester the casting director more than once, as this can result in your untimely death.

Another way of finding out about castings is by hanging around some of the trendy 'actor' clubs in town like The Groucho, Soho House or The Ivy. If you can't afford the expensive membership fees, befriend a member of the club and go as a guest, or climb in via the fire escape. Once inside, put on a nice tight T-shirt, and do a little bit of detective work to track down the important people. If you don't know what the 'important' people look like, you can always sniff them out. Important theatre people have two smells: sweet and powerful (think cinnamon, leather and dark chocolate); and old and musty (think Lloyd Webber's underwear). However, if you go as a guest you can avoid the 'sniffing' by asking your host to introduce you to the important people. If you are lucky enough to meet, say, a director, you must always try and remain calm. Sweating, shaking or vomiting is to be avoided. Particularly if the director is wearing a nice suit from M&S.

If you are speaking to a director at a social event, just chat to them like you would to anyone else. Mention that you're an actor only *once*, at the beginning of the conversation, but that's it. Never revert back to the fact that you are an actor again. Always ask them how they are, what they are doing, what television programmes they like, and what they think of Denise Welch and Russell Crowe. This will get them speaking to you on a one-to-one level, and start to feel relaxed around you. At this stage I recommend buying them several drinks and getting them savagely sloshed. By the time they sober up you'll have all their contact details and some very embarrassing photos of them. You are sure to get an audition now, dear.

Good Audition Tips

In your audition you should aim to be professional at all times. But whilst being professional, never change who you are. You have been brought into the room because the casting director wants to see you – so already they are interested. Let this give you confidence. It may also be useful to try and not imagine it as an audition. Imagine that you are going into a room to explore a character – it is a chance to be creative and offer something original and unique to the panel. If you go in there feeling like you are a good actor who wants to show their craft, as opposed to a person going in to audition against a load of other actors, you may find the whole thing more enjoyable. However, if all this sounds too much like hard work, have a swig of vodka.

Body Contact

Should you shake my hand when you enter? I honestly don't mind if you do, but please make sure that your hand has been recently cleaned. I appreciate that many actors get nervous and go to the toilet directly before auditioning, but I'm not always sure if they've washed their hands afterwards. I'm not a massive fan of body contact anyway, and the thought of shaking a toilet-infected hand makes me want to hug my Jean Valjean teddy. I shall start asking all actors to sanitise their hands when they enter the audition room. That way everyone involved can feel relaxed that hands are bacteria-free. This is the reason I now wear gloves whenever I'm in public. It makes everything much more hygienic. And makes me feel like the Queen, dear.

You should *never* attempt to kiss anyone on the audition panel – unless they go to kiss you first. If this happens, you are legally obliged to follow through and kiss them back. However, you must never, ever stick your tongue in. This smacks of overenthusiasm and can leave a bitter taste in the mouth. Particularly if you've been eating cheese and onion crisps.

The same applies with a hug. If a casting director goes to hug you, you must politely comply. Even if they smell of wee and mothballs. There is an unwritten theatrical law which states that actors should always be prepared to hug, fondle or gently caress casting directors if they really want the job. If you are extra lucky you may even be offered a 'happy ending'. Or, even worse, an unhappy ending.

Illness

At the beginning of your audition, please don't tell the panel that you're ill. Unless they can actually see a flesh wound, or you have a valid doctor's note, they will presume you felt underprepared and are lying. It's not good enough. We had an actor in last year who looked as pale as one of those *Twilight* actors – but when he started singing he sweated and his white make-up started falling off his face. Michael Ball has thankfully never tried that since. However, if you are genuinely ill then it's your own fault. You're an actor – you're not allowed to get ill.

Enthusiasm

I always like to remind actors not to seem overly keen. Enthusiasm is a great thing, and is what drives us to be the best at what we do. But overenthusiasm is a killer. It makes actors seem desperate and weak. Having a constant fake smile is never a good sign. I can appreciate good teeth, but when you audition for me, chances are we are not casting for the new Colgate campaign. I say 'just be yourself'. Be interested and professional, but not keen and needy. I find it ridiculous when actors constantly smile through their songs. Think about the character. If you are singing 'Javert's Suicide' it really isn't helpful to see your lovely white veneers, dear.

Standing

It can be very embarrassing if you stand in the wrong place and look uncomfortable. I suggest you stand facing the audition panel (i.e. not with your back to them). Make sure you aren't too close, but if you suffer from halitosis or tend to dribble then it's a good idea to stand even further back. Make sure you feel nice and relaxed before you start to perform, because if you look nervous, you sound nervous.

Excessive vibrato does not hide bad singing, dear.

The Singing Audition

Before you start singing, remember that you have to be in character from the beginning. When you hear the pianist playing those ominous first notes, your performance has begun. Never spend the song's intro smiling at the panel like you are a Barry Manilow impersonator, and don't start doing bizarre yoga stretches. If in doubt, take the 'neutral vacant-stare pose' that actors are very good at. It makes you look harmless, vulnerable and dull all at the same time. Which is exactly the kind of actor that directors like to work with.

As a general rule, when we ask you to sing we don't want a piece of tightly rehearsed choreography to go along with it. We just want to hear your voice. Invariably the dancing will just distract and you'll end up looking like an inferior Strallen sister. We had an actor audition recently who did some marvellous split jumps and ball-changes, but was so out of breath by the chorus he couldn't sing. And, to be honest, the choreography didn't really go with 'Memory' anyway, dear.

If I want you to give me eye contact when you are singing, I will ask. But if I do, please don't think that means you should wink at me in any part of your song. Winking will result in one thing – me drawing a naughty body part all over your headshot.

I often hear actors moaning about what the panel are doing when they sing. I try and remain as attentive as I can, but like anyone, I get distracted. If you perform a song like 'Corner of the Sky' that I have heard fifteen times that day, I am going to reach for my iPhone and start playing Angry Birds. I'm not being rude – I'm just saving my sanity. If you sing a song really well, and I think you show a lot of potential, I will usually watch you for a while, and then finish drawing a picture of Sarah Brightman on my notepad. I rarely make notes about what you sing; I tend to see who you remind me of – and that's what I write. If you remind me of someone like Colm Wilkinson or Jonathan Pryce then you get a recall. But if you remind me of Amanda Holden then you're doomed to be working front of house for another year.

There has always been a misconception about what it means if we ask you to sing a second song. To be honest, it depends. If we are bored with your first song but think you looked right and sounded good, we won't bother asking you to sing again, we'll just recall you. If your first song was fine, but didn't show the range we want, we'll ask you to sing again. And if your first song was really bad, we'll ask you to do another one just to keep us amused. One of my casting directors is terrible – he always asks the boys he fancies to sing two songs, just so he can drool a little longer. I've told him to stop doing this, but bless him, it's one of the only kicks he gets these days.

There's nothing as upsetting as a half-hearted ball-change, dear.

The Dance Audition

I'm a big admirer of actors who can dance. It is a discipline I have never mastered myself; indeed, the closest thing I can do that even slightly resembles dancing is a few ball-changes. And even then I get all my balls mixed up, dear.

When auditioning for a dance show, the panel are on the lookout for highly skilled and bendy dancers. Personally, I love nothing more than watching a good tap routine, or a dancer who can get their leg over their shoulder and hold it there long enough for us to stare at their groin region. It really is thrilling. However, many choreographers I know are far more interested in skill, technique, charisma and personality. The secret to dancing is making it look easy. If you can do a triple pirouette, peel a potato, balance an ensemble member on your forehead and look relaxed all at the same time, you will never be out of work. And, indeed, those times when you are out of work you will be able to get some well-paid specialised dancing work in Soho.

Dance auditions are pretty straightforward affairs. We generally cram as many dancers as possible into a room the size of a telephone box and make them copy the choreographer. As a rule, this session will be taken by the choreographer's assistant – allowing the actual choreographer to sit behind a table and touch himself. It is a lot safer having the assistants run these auditions as they tend to be far more talented than the choreographers themselves.

The dance will be taught – and everyone will be expected to remember it instantly. If you are one of those people who find it hard to pick up moves, you will be told that it doesn't matter and will be given more time. Of course, this is a lie – because in dance, speed is essential (unless you've been on a reality TV show, in which case, we'll just make everyone else dance around you).

Never stand at the back of the room during a dance call. If you do, you will not have a very good view of the choreography, and will inevitably start copying the person in front of you – who will be making it up. Standing at the back also gives the impression that you are scared. Never let the audition panel know that you are scared. Unless Louie Spence is running the audition. Then I'd be scared too, dear.

Having been taught the dance, and practised it a few times, you will be split into groups and asked to perform the choreography. If you are smart you will have been looking around the room to spot which dancers are the worst and planted yourself in the middle of them. This increases your chances of looking good.

After performing the set choreography you may be asked to show us some 'freestyle'. This means doing some dance moves of your own – with the aim of showing your skills to the best of your ability. If ever the choreographer tells you that they are looking for 'style' and not 'tricks', do not believe them. We are *always* looking for tricks. If you can do some neat headstands, belly flops, or simply dazzle us with some impressive magic tricks, you will always get a recall. Never be shy. Show off!

Sometimes we rename the 'dance call' and call it the 'movement call'. This is to make actors who are not very confident at dancing come along. The term 'movement' sounds a lot less threatening than 'dance', and implies that all that is required is some stretches and silly jumping around. In truth, however, the choreography in a movement call is exactly the same as that of a dance call, only slightly slower.

If you have done enough to impress us – and get offered the job in a dance show, then you have to be clever. If you want an easy few months in the show, you should not offer too many tricks or anything difficult in the first few weeks of rehearsals. This will ensure the choreographer puts you at the back and gives you the simpler stuff. Of course, the same applies to physical-theatre pieces – never offer too much. You always have to think about the effect of doing the same thing night after night after night.

It may sound absurd me advising you to look after yourself – but to be honest I suggest it for purely selfish reasons. The main one being that it can get bloody expensive paying for actors to go to a physio or massage therapist every week due to an injury sustained during the show. I would much prefer you did something a little easier on your body so it avoids me the unnecessary expense of having to pay for your body to be realigned. Of course, if you have an injury as a direct result of the show we will always look after you and make sure you return to the world in the same condition as when we stole you from it.

However, if you have a pre-existing condition, we are not obliged to look after that part of your body. For example, I heard of a young man in *Avenue Q* who constantly complained about his hand and wrist being in severe pain due to the puppets – so he was duly booked in to see a physiotherapist. Two weeks later a colleague revealed that this actor had the same injury on every single job he did, and that it had nothing to do with the puppets – he just used to spend an awful lot of time touching his naughty bits. And as much as I understand the temptation to do this, I refuse to pay for self-induced kinky injuries of this sort.

Actors – to be viewed as an actor-musician in auditions, take a trumpet, blow hard, and hope for the best, dear.

The Informal Chat

At the end of your audition we will have a little chat about what you've been up to recently. This is your chance to tell us all about yourself, ask questions, and allows my casting director to find out if you're gay.

When we ask what you've been doing recently, we're not enquiring about your recent holiday or stamp collection. We're actually asking about your last few acting jobs. And if you haven't done any recent acting jobs then just say you're in the process of devising a piece about cottage cheese or something. It makes you sound a lot more interesting, dear.

And finally, when you leave the audition – please be careful never to slam the door. That's very dangerous as it could wake me up.

Bad Audition Habits

There are lots of obvious things that actors should avoid doing in an audition, like turning up drunk and or turning up late. But there are also some less obvious steps that should be considered. One of them is what to wear.

Men

Never wear trousers that are too thin. Today's fashion sense astounds me. I do not understand why people with bandy, breakable legs would want every inch of their twiglet calves to be shown. It is most upsetting. I tend to sit behind my table thanking the lord that my own trousers allow my legs to breathe. Similarly, it is not good highlighting your panty region, no matter how big your appendage appears to be. When watching a lovely rendition of 'Martin Guerre', it is never nice to see an auditionee's testicles retract on the high G at the end. That's a big no-no, dear.

I would advise men to wear smart-casual clothing that is loose and allows you to move well (by 'loose', I don't mean having your jeans halfway down your legs – I have no interest in seeing your underwear). If your outfit can make you look a little like the role you are up for then this is beneficial, as it makes the casting director's job easier. For example, if you are coming in for the role of Jean Valjean I would recommend a nice beard, a loaf of bread, and some ripped, dirty clothes. And if you are up for Javert it would be nice to see your truncheon.

It is advisable to wear a scarf or theatrical cravate when auditioning for roles at the RSC and National. They love that sort of thing, dear.

I would also suggest you show the panel as many different 'looks' as you have. So if you have glasses, wear them at the beginning of your audition and take them off halfway through. A subtler way of showing us your 'glasses face' is by putting them on when reading the script. Also, for women, if your hair is long, tie it in a bun at the beginning, and then let it flow beautifully down at some point. If gentlemen are particularly keen to impress, they can start an audition with a beard, and shave it off during their first song.

Women

I don't mind you wearing heels, but please don't wear heels that totally change the way you look. I saw an actress once who walked like she was auditioning to be a one-legged pirate. When I asked her if she'd be more comfortable with her shoes off she said, 'No. My heels give me confidence.' On her CV it said she was four foot two; in her heels she looked like an Amazonian she-male.

I would advise women, like men, to wear smart-casual clothing. If you want to get more dressed up I would only suggest this on your first audition, as the second one usually involves more movement. You should always make sure that your hair is tied back, or at least make sure it's not hiding your face (unless you are using your hair to cover up a particularly violent spot). Also avoid wearing too much jewellery as it distracts my casting director, who will spend the entire audition wondering where you got it from. It is especially important that you don't wear big hoop earrings, particularly for a dance audition, as they make you look like a TV aerial, and we don't want someone getting caught up in them and ripping your ear off. It is also useful to wear a skirt that is adjustable, so if you spot the director staring at your legs you can lift your skirt a little and tease. Obviously this technique is a little naughty, but can have delicious results if you are creative. I remember an audition where a cheeky actress lifted her skirt slightly to reveal her headshot which was stuck to her thigh. Sadly she didn't get the job. But she did get a rather rewarding workshop with the director that evening, dear.

So, in retrospect, my main pieces of advice when auditioning are: don't drink, don't shout, don't dance, don't wink at me, don't wear tight trousers or high heels, don't smile too much, and always wash your hands. Basically – be professional and be yourself. After all, it is a job interview, dear.

Getting an Offer

The highlight of an actor's life is getting the job. Sadly, it's all downhill from there. Being offered a job validates you as an actor. You feel wanted, important, successful and powerful. And so you should. It's difficult getting any job these days – particularly an acting one. There is nothing as marvellous as being told by your agent that 'You've got an offer.' And always remember that. This is the one time when you have some power. The casting director, director, and me, the producer, want *you*. We need *you* to help make the show work.

When you receive an offer you have some bargaining power. The first thing to do is consider if you actually want the role. If you've been through the pain and suffering of the audition process I can only imagine you must at least be interested in the show. If you are one of those actors that just go to auditions to meet the casting director regardless of whether you want the job or not – take it from me: don't bother. Nothing will anger a casting director, director and producer more than if you go through five auditions only for us to find out that you weren't interested in the first place. It is infuriating, and can lead to severe rumours about your professionalism and your personal life spreading around every casting department in the West End.

Hopefully you will be ecstatic about being offered the role. However, we never expect actors to accept the job straight away. Their agent will usually play 'hard to get' for the next few weeks – and tell us that their client is 'considering the role' or has 'been offered something else so is weighing up the options'. This is all well and good – but we're not stupid. We're perfectly aware that your agent is just telling us a silly little lie to make you sound popular. Which can be dangerous. Because if you 'weigh up' my offer for too long, you might as well forget it. I know many actors who have had offers withdrawn because of the ridiculous games that agents play with us.

Actors – at the end of your audition, please avoid saying 'See you later.' Because chances are, you won't, dear.

ACT TWO: REHEARSING

OR
GESTURING, GIGGLING, GURNING, GOOGLING, GESTICULATING, GROVELLING AND GROWING

Every time someone says 'I don't believe in jazz hands', an actor dies. Do your bit. And believe, dear.

Rehearsing

A word of warning: Sometimes I get reports of actors spending all their time munching on my chocolate HobNobs in rehearsals, and after four weeks of this it adds an unnecessary expense on my show budget. The respectful actor should limit their HobNob intake to one a day. But most do not. This has caused me to request my company manager take a tally of how many HobNobs actors eat every day. And if you eat more than two, you certainly won't be working for me again, dear.

The First Day

Most directors like to start day one of rehearsals with a 'meet and greet' – where everyone is invited to turn up wearing something flattering to impress their fellow cast members, and decide who they want to sleep with. During this time everyone will be asked to sit in a circle and introduce themselves. This is where actors realise how important the circle-sitting term is at drama school.

Circle-sitting

Circle-sitting has many mystic secrets – and, if performed badly, can lead to depression, fatigue, and in severe cases, death. There are many elements to consider: Who do you sit next to? Do you start the circle? Do you place your bag under your seat or at the side? Do you cross your legs? Do you fold your arms? Do you have a 'Sharon Stone *Basic Instinct*' moment? Overall it takes a lot of pre-planning and thorough investigation to answer these important questions. But once you have decided where to sit, never change your mind – as this shows you only did a one-year training course.

Sitting next to the director has many advantages. It allows you to see their script and notes, and more importantly it allows you to smell them. Smelling your director is vitally important – it will tell you how good they are. If they smell fresh and gorgeous, chances are they are only eighteen and this is their first job. If they smell of chocolate and marshmallows, chances are they have only ever directed children's theatre. If they smell of alcohol, cigarettes and wee, chances are they are very good. And if they smell sweaty and rusty, chances are they are Trevor Nunn.

After the circle-sitting trauma you will be asked to introduce yourselves. Always remember that it is advisable to do this in your own accent, with as little dribbling as possible. I also advise saying your first name first, followed by your surname. You're not James Bond, dear.

After introducing themselves, actors sometimes feel the need to talk about their previous acting roles. This is a waste of time as the other actors have already stalked you on Spotlight and found out all your credits anyway.

The Introduction

Next usually comes a nice introduction by the set designer. Set designers are flamboyantly dressed people who stand at the back in loafers. They are quietly confident individuals who arrive with their own secret weapon: the model-box. Set designers love showing their box. The model-box is a little cardboard theatre, and in it are placed various bits of set. A well-known actor once got very confused by this tradition – thinking he was going to be performing in a theatre the size of a Corn Flakes box. Bless Brian Blessed, he gets dazed when he hasn't had a bar of Dairy Milk before 10 a.m., dear.

The set designer then puts his little box on a table, and everyone applauds enthusiastically as though he has just cured the common cold. Then actors are expected to stare at it and yelp excitedly as each new bit of set is added. The designer will go into detail about each scene, and move little toy army soldiers around the box to convey the actors. On many occasions the toy soldiers are actually far better at acting than the actors we've employed.

Sometimes the director will interject with ideas about the set, and why he has decided to set *Hamlet* on the moon – and both designer and director will go to great lengths to justify their vision. It is at this point that the actors look concerned, and wish they were back in *Hollyoaks* discussing teenage pregnancy and alcopops.

The designer will then show sketches of the costumes he has in mind. This is the point when you can tell who the designer a) dislikes, and b) fancies. The people he fancies will have all the lovely frocks, and the most complimentary suits. The actors he doesn't like are invariably made to look like old, withered scabs. Over the years I have seen many fine actors reduced to gibbering wrecks when they realise they are going to spend five months in Westcliff-on-Sea dressed as a six-foot fungal disorder.

And then it is lunch.

At lunch you either disappear on your own and make important-looking phone calls (which usually means you are calling your agent to get you out of the contract) – or you try and be social and go for a pub lunch with everyone else, with the aim of figuring out who is a friend or foe. As a general rule, friendly actors will order scampi and chips, and difficult actors will order trout.

The Warm-up

Sometimes a full-company warm-up is made compulsory in the afternoon and everyone has to take part. The warm-up will consist of movement, vocal exercises, trust games or group sex. One company at Stratford in the sixties failed to rehearse anything as they spent the whole time copulating. Marvellous for them, but terrible for the Cub Scout Pack next door.

I often find that actors treat the company warm-up as a competition. They will wear the skimpiest outfits and tightest T-shirts available. Whilst I admire people's physical attributes, I never feel the need to be punished by seeing someone's nipple rings or Prince Albert. Some things are just left better to the imagination. At one warm-up recently a female was dressed in such tiny hot pants that her lady region kept winking at me, dear.

This is also where another standard 'actor rule' comes into play: the water bottle. To be a proper actor it is vital that you attend rehearsals with one. It is a serious offence not to hold a water bottle at least once during a rehearsal day – and is seen as an act of rebellion if no water is consumed. Water is a marvellous tool. It provides you with essential nutrients and hydrates your body. It also makes you need the toilet on a regular basis – which is essential for checking your make-up, checking your sweat patches and allowing the boys to stuff extra toilet paper down their pants. Also, a water bottle is the perfect place to hide gin.

The Readthrough

At some stage on the first day of rehearsals, scripts will be taken out, and directors will indulge themselves by having a readthrough. Many directors say that you shouldn't treat the readthrough as 'a performance' – it is just about 'listening to the story'. That's a lie. The readthrough is basically another audition – where the director and producer sit there thinking: 'Come on then, I've employed you. Prove that we've made the right decision.' Invariably we have, but on those occasions where we've made a mistake, I have the Krankies on speed-dial just in case.

Many actors treat their script like a Bible. They bind it in a leather folder, christen it at a place of worship and, in extreme cases, sleep with it. I don't find it problematic when actors sleep with their scripts – but I do feel sorry for their partners. I heard of one actor who got so involved with his script that he dressed it up in a mini-skirt and took it out for a meal at Jamie's Italian. I wouldn't have minded but it was the script for a Theatre in Education tour of *Thomas and the Fat Controller: A Love Story*. Hardly Shakespeare, dear.

....

To be a proper actor it is essential you have a leather binder to put your scripts in, dear.

....

Standing Up and Trying to Act

When proper rehearsals finally begin, the director will usually tell you where to stand and how to say your lines. Some of these new 'arty' directors will allow the actors to 'discover' their moves and dialogue, but this is a complete waste of time. It's a lot easier when the actors just do exactly what they are told, and stand and move when instructed to do so. In fact, there was a study done by a university recently about what kind of direction is more effective: 'The director using the actors as robots' versus 'The actors being creative and finding meaning and validity in the play.' Obviously 'actors as robots' was far more cost-effective – as it meant a play could be put on in two weeks as opposed to two months.

Some directors I have employed like to spend a lot of time sitting at a table and discussing the play with their actors. This approach only takes place when actors can read and have been to Oxford or Cambridge – and generally only happens at the RSC.

Actors should never be afraid of saying what they think about a scene and play. But they should never actually say it in rehearsals. It's far healthier to keep all their thoughts to themselves and reveal them *only* when in a pub with other actors. Usually everyone else will agree with these thoughts, but actors are not paid to have ideas. That is what the Assistant Stage Manager is for, dear.

Three-act plays are a lot better without the second one, dear.

The Types of Actors

Every company you are part of becomes like living in a 'bubble' with a different dynamic and a different energy – and after a few days your status in this new group will be decided. However, in each job you can actually decide to be a different kind of person, a different personality – and this can make the job even more enjoyable, and even more naughty. Most people have one first day at work. Actors have hundreds.

The nine different 'types' in an acting company are:

The Leader – This is the person or persons who are playing the leading roles. They have a desire and responsibility to lead the company in every aspect – both in the theatre, and in the pub afterwards. They are expected to buy lots of drinks for the rest of the company and pay at least fifty per cent of any company meal.

The Comedian – The person who makes a joke out of every situation. The comedian is rather fun during the rehearsal period, but tends to turn into a depressed alcoholic mess in the second month of the run.

The Sex Pest – This person constantly talks about sex and attempts to sleep with anyone and everyone in the company. They will usually be in a relationship, and are firm believers in the 'It doesn't count on tour' rule. They will also attend monthly seminars held by Leslie Grantham and Steve McFadden.

The Teacher's Pet – This person will do whatever they are told by anyone who says it. They will be highly skilled in laughing at the director's jokes, and will be the first person in the rehearsal room. The sex pest will try their luck with this person in week one as they seem the most impressionable. But they are not. They are just highly skilled at 'playing the game'.

The Rebel – This person will always try and be Equity Deputy and stand up for actors' rights. They will be very verbal about their thoughts on any situation, whether they know what they're talking about or not. It is easiest just to smile and agree with them. If they are provoked they will talk for hours, and turn many a good drinking night into a heated political debate. When this happens simply hand them a copy of the Equity Rulebook and ask them what came first – Equity or Acting.

The Dominatrix – Exactly the same as the sex pest, but owns a whip.

The Juve – The 'juve' refers to the juvenile lead – or youngest person in the company. These people tend to have a 28-inch waist and a nice complexion. They will be the newest and freshest person in the company – and will enter the rehearsal room with grand ideas and obscure acting methods. For the sanity of the rest of the company it is essential these ideas are knocked out of them by day two.

The Mother – This person likes to care for and support the rest of the company. It will usually be a lady in her mid-forties to late fifties, who wears at least a 36DD bra. The mother is a popular company member, and will earn points by bringing in biscuits and cakes for the rest of the company.

The Company Idiot – There is always one member of the company who is known as the idiot. If you don't know who this person is, then it is you.

Within the first week of rehearsals you should be able to spot who is who from the above list. If you know what person you usually are, I suggest trying to be someone else. For example, if you are usually the sex pest try being the mother instead. It will be a marvellous new experience for you. I adore watching rehearsals and picking out which actor is the dominatrix – it gives me and my casting director hours of fun.

When an actor says 'I've not got many lines, but I'm in a lot of scenes', it means they look nice but aren't very good.

Building a Character

Throughout your professional life – and at drama school – you will frequently be asked to think about your *character*. This does not mean thinking about your own personality, but is a challenge to work on the role that you are playing. There are many workshops out there that claim to help with this mystical and challenging art form – some are good, some are bad, and some are very ugly indeed.

I have been lucky enough to spend lots of Dom-filled evenings with many directors. And whilst I generally try to avoid talking about work, invariably we end up in long discussions about it. Only last week I was discussing 'character work' with a very well-known director. He shared the following thoughts with me before vomiting on my Mister Mistoffelees rug.

One of the best ways of learning about your character is by reading the script and discovering what your character says. If your character says nothing then chances are you are a mute or a mime artist. If this is the case then you will have a nice easy rehearsal period. If you are a central character in the script you will have lots of dialogue – and in all of this dialogue there will be lots of hints about your character. However, I do realise that this kind of research is hard – particularly for those actors that cannot read. In those instances I recommend asking your mummy to do it for you.

Some people, like David Mamet, are of the belief that you should simply say the lines and the character will appear. By this he means that the writer has already created the character, and the actor's job is just to deliver the dialogue. This is an interesting idea, but is no use at all if you are playing an animal that just barks. This is where 'animal studies' can prove very useful.

If you are playing an animal then you should go and study that animal. If you've been to drama school you will undoubtedly have done an 'animal studies' term – where you all smell each other and pretend to be Doctor Dolittle. As I'm sure you're aware, animal studies is not just a case of sitting down and copying the animal – you have to get inside the 'animal's head'. You have to think like the animal, behave like the animal, and procreate like the animal. There was a production of *The Wind in the Willows* in the late seventies where the entire cast lived on a river for a month. It was great for their characters, and they all really understood their animals, but the show had to be completely recast as they all contracted Weil's disease.

You may also find animals useful in informing the human character you are playing. For example, imagine what kind of animal your character is – and use the animal to aid your choices about the mannerisms, physicality and vocal qualities of your character. What kind of an animal do you imagine Hamlet to be? Is he a dog, a giraffe, a humpback whale? For my money he's something like a Golden Retriever – an animal that is quiet, loyal, pensive, and nice to stroke. However, I have seen some productions of Hamlet where the actor playing him obviously thought he was an elephant as he plodded, shouted, dribbled, got on all fours, and even got his trunk out. But I suppose that serves me right for going to an after-midnight version of *Hamlet* at the Edinburgh Festival, dear.

Actors like Daniel Day-Lewis believe they should constantly be *in character* – and insist on being in character off-set as well as on. This is fine if you are living near the set and the whole cast and crew are aware of it. It does, however, get a little more complicated when you are starring in a musical and randomly burst into song during your weekly shop at Tesco. Of course, there is nothing to stop you attempting this method – but always remember that police will not accept 'I was in character' as a valid excuse for stealing a MacBook Pro.

Personally, I think one of the most effective ways of building a character is by purchasing a DVD of the film or stage version of the show that your character is from (or go and watch it at the theatre if it is already on). This is particularly useful when taking over a role in a cast change as it saves my resident director days of valuable rehearsal time. Of course, in Stanislavsky's time this option wasn't available, but if he were around today I'm sure he would applaud this instinctive method. Copying is the highest form of flattery – and if another artist has already tackled the role then there is no reason why you shouldn't use his version as a guide. I wouldn't suggest copying the entire performance – purely for legal reasons – but if you wear some glasses and a beard to make yourself look different then you should be fine.

Actors – never disagree with your director. Just agree and then forget, dear.

Acting in a Serious Play

A serious play will often have a sofa, a drinks cabinet, a large space in the middle in which actors are allowed to walk and talk, and an ashtray. This setting is the default for many serious plays – as it allows lots of random lounging, perching, walking in the middle, stirring of liquids, and contemplative cigarette-smoking.

A serious actor has to approach acting in a serious way. This can be achieved by using various methods. One of the easiest ways is by not smiling – particularly if you don't have good teeth. A serious actor should always save his smile for special occasions. However, this does not mean you can't smirk. Smirking and smiling are two very different things indeed.

You should adopt an expression that makes you look permanently interested, as though you are always considering something. This will give everyone the impression you are constantly thinking about something to do with the play – when in fact you are just considering whether to have a kebab on your way home.

When speaking to other actors or the director, the serious actor will always speak slowly and take lots of pauses. Never be ashamed of pauses – they make you appear strong. In fact, sometimes it is rather fun to see how long you can get away with a pause – by pretending that you are searching for a specific word. Always maintain eye contact and use long and complicated words. Examples of impressive words to use are: 'characterisation', 'development', 'historically', 'gonorrhoea', 'establishment', 'accurate', 'nautical' and 'hummus'. Of course, you will never be expected to use all of these words in the same sentence, but it is amazing how you can make anything sound intriguing: 'My development of gonorrhoea in the characterisation with regards to the establishment is not historically accurate, particularly when the play is nautical. Hummus, anyone?'

A cleft in the chin can also be very useful as it makes you look like a relative of Kirk Douglas. And he is marvellous.

Acting is the art of reacting. So make sure you do a lot of it, dear.

The Shoe Method

Dedicated serious actors will own a pair or strong boots or suede loafers. Serious actors always have one or the other, depending on what mood they are in. In fact, just like an actor can find a character by wearing the right shoes, a person can find what kind of actor they are by the shoes they are wearing.

The shoe method is very useful, particularly for the new actor. It can provide an instant feeling of 'belonging', particularly when you spot other actors wearing the same footwear as you.

Musical-theatre footwear – A Capezio, tap shoe, ballet shoe, or any brightly coloured trainer. Musical-theatre actors need to be able to adapt to different styles of dancing and performance – and must always be prepared with different types of shoes. It is usual to hear a collective 'groan' when a company of dancers are told they are going to be doing some tap. Inwardly, however, they are all delighted, as it allows them to wear their tap shoes again. It is essential that musical-theatre footwear is easy to move in, allowing quick escapes from perverted choreographers.

Physical-theatre footwear – No footwear needed. Physical-theatre performers like to feel the ground beneath them as it gives them an 'earthy' performance. Of course, this does carry health risks, and the spreading of athlete's foot and verrucas is well documented in physical-theatre companies.

Serious actor footwear – A boot or a suede loafer. They should be comfortable, and have an air of authority about them. Men should never wear a heel over the height of four inches as this suggests that you like cross-dressing in your spare time.

Leading actor's footwear – Any shoe, trainer or boot that doesn't require you to wear socks. A sockless performer is always the lead performer, dear.

Actors – taking long pauses during your speech does not make it better. It just makes it longer, dear.

Acting Through Song

Singing is hard enough on its own, but sometimes you will be asked to act at the same time. Many people don't believe that singing and acting should be attempted simultaneously but it is very popular with audiences at present, and producers are prepared to pay the big bucks for it. If you are a performer who can act, dance and sing you could be earning as much as Equity minimum, which is around £420 a week on tour (plus £210 subsistence). If you are in the West End we are forced to pay you even more – approximately £510 in the small West End theatres (more in larger houses). Which is a huge amount of money. Particularly for someone who went to drama school for three years, is classed as a skilled professional, and has a family and mortgage to pay for. However, many unfortunate actors never make it to this prestigious position – and spend their lives claiming squatters' rights in English Heritage properties whilst performing in profit-share productions.

The first thing to do when tackling a song is to learn the correct tune. Look at the sheet music, follow the dots, and sing *exactly* what is written. Look at the punctuation of the lyrics, and treat them as if they are a speech. Think about the character's situation, who they are singing to, and what effect they are trying to convey. Another very useful tool is to think about breathing. It is no good singing the entire song on one breath as this will result in death. So go through the song and mark on the sheet music the best times to breathe. Make sure your breath doesn't come in the middle of important phrases and split up the journey of the song.

Always be aware of your eyebrows. Frequently I see overactive eyebrows ruin a beautiful performance. Eyebrows are tools used to shield the eyes from sweat and rain. They are not an acting tool – unless you are John Barrowman. If your eyebrows have a habit of uncontrollably moving up and down when you sing, the best thing to do is to staple them in place. However, if you can't tolerate this kind of pain then you should just sing in front of a mirror. Every time your eyebrows make an involuntary movement, stop singing and try that section again – until your eyebrows settle down. Once you achieve 'eyebrow peace', the number of castings you get will double.

Some songs are sung directly to the audience – a solo song – where the character is left on stage to sing through their thoughts. Examples of this kind of song are: 'On My Own', 'Starlight Express' and 'Gangnam Style'. These songs typically require more concentration – as you have to master the 'staring vacantly out front' technique. This technique is very valuable in both solo songs and when performing with actors who are crap (craptors, see page 66) – indeed, this technique will prove a valuable tool in all future work you do.

All you need to do is allow your eyes to glaze over, and stare directly out front as you sing. The odd eye movement is an interesting little bonus – I suggest looking to the upper circle in wonderment a couple of times, and then back down. Halfway through the song I recommend a small hand gesture. In fact, if you are feeling extra brave and fancy being nominated for an Olivier Award, you can attempt the 'Evita double-hand stretch'. However, this should only be used on special occasions as it is exhausting. There will obviously come a key change towards the end of the song, which is when you should take two or three steps forward, being careful not to fall into the orchestra pit. On the last line of the song look pleadingly around the auditorium and, if on the final note you can bite your tongue and make yourself cry, you will be heavily praised. And it's a simple as that.

Of course, if you can't be bothered to do any of the above just listen to the CD and copy it.

....

When singing high notes it should feel free and easy. You generally know you've done something wrong if you shit yourself, dear.

....

Accents

Often in acting jobs you will be required not only to talk, but also to do it in a funny voice (or 'accent' as it is known in the trade). An accent is the way someone talks from a specific part of the world – and if you are very good at them you can get yourself a lot of work. However, if you can't do accents you can just cultivate your own voice until it is so distinctive it becomes an accent in its own right. Take Alan Rickman and Judi Dench – the only accent they ever do is their own. And quite right too, dear.

Even if you are awful at accents it is still expected that you put 'good ear for accents' on your CV. This is something that actors are told to do in their final term at drama school. To be honest, if we want a specific accent we'll hire an actor who is from that part of the world anyway. Either that or we'll see if Alistair McGowan is available.

In the old days, drama schools used to knock actors' regional accents out of them and make everyone speak in RP. RP stands for 'received pronunciation' or 'really posh'. Actors are always expected to have a good RP accent, preparing them for work by Shakespeare, Chekhov and Julian Fellowes. These days, however, actors are positively encouraged to retain their regional accents, as it improves their chances of getting roles in more highbrow shows like *Hollyoaks* and *Emmerdale*.

There are even some companies that tour Shakespeare with an all-Northern cast. I think this is marvellous, and makes Shakespeare's language much more accessible for today's audiences. There is nothing lovelier than overhearing an audience member saying 'I never knew Shakespeare wrote *Coronation Street.*' Bless, dear.

The best way to learn a new accent is by observing someone who speaks with the accent you desire – and copy them. Watch the way their mouth moves, their lips, observe the placement of their tongue, and how nasal the sound is. It is also useful to consider the physicality of someone, as this can have a direct effect on an accent. For example, if some-one has really stiff shoulders it will have a direct effect on the tightness of their voice.

Always make sure you stretch well before attempting an accent. This is particularly important when trying Welsh, dear.

Upstaging

Upstaging is a term that terrifies actors. It refers to an actor who moves upstage of another actor, forcing the first actor to face away from the audience. As an example, imagine an actress is singing centre-stage to another actor, and the other actor positions himself towards the back of the stage (upstage). This forces the actress to sing her song upstage to him, in the opposite direction of the audience. It is a very clever trick that can make an inexperienced actor do their entire performance facing the back wall.

There have been numerous stories of actors constantly upstaging their colleagues, in an attempt to make sure they get all the attention. You should always be on the lookout for such actors – and put a stop to it as quickly and violently as possible. If they start doing it in rehearsals the director will notice and exert necessary discipline on the guilty actor. However, the more experienced actor will only start upstag-ing during performances, at which point the director will have left.

Not that I condone it, but if you are ever working with some-one you don't like, upstaging is a marvellous way of starting an argument. And the same applies to lights. There are many ways of 'stealing an actor's light' – the simplest by blocking their light (which is particularly easy to do when the light is coming from the side of the stage). All you have to do is stand directly in front of the light that is lighting the actor, and he will be forced to perform in darkness. It is a very naughty trick, but one which can be delicious fun during matinees in Bognor.

I remember an astonishing instance of upstaging a few years ago when two leading performers began upstaging each other. As the scene went on, each stubbornly carried on with his upstaging by taking one step further towards the back of the stage – until finally both of them were backed against the far wall shouting at each other. It was the fiercest onstage tantrum between two divas I have ever witnessed. And marked the end of Cannon and Ball's working relationship. So terribly sad, dear.

....

Please avoid spitting and dribbling when performing. I have just had a face wash listening to someone singing 'Why God Why?', dear.

....

Learning Lines

Line-learning is something I do not envy. I have witnessed many actors attempting different and interesting techniques over the years – with varying degrees of success. In truth, one of the most effective ways of learning lines is simply by going through them as often as possible. This is known in the business as the 'parrot fashion' technique.

However, there are other more experimental methods, some of which allegedly speed up this arduous process.

One of the most risky is the 'not learning your lines' method. The actor who adopts this technique will hope and pray that during rehearsals the lines will organically enter their memory, so that they don't actually have to do any learning at home. And, indeed, for some actors this technique works triumphantly. They have an inherent gift for remembering lines, and find the whole task ridiculously easy. These kinds of people tend to be rather lucky and have a photographic memory. In fact, one of my dear friends has a photographic memory. I've always tried to convince her to remember the *Complete Works of Shakespeare* – so that she becomes an invaluable asset to the RSC. She said there was no point as she doesn't understand any of his plays. I told her that no one really does, dear.

Another, rather more experimental method is to record your lines and listen back to them as often as possible – whether this be on a train, bus, underground or at a swimming pool. Wherever, and whenever possible – the point is you just listen and listen and listen. Many people find playing their lines on a loop just before going to bed rather useful – so that they play continuously as you sleep. This way is apparently very effective as it allows the lines to enter your head subconsciously. However, I have heard horror stories of actors who have tried this and ended up only knowing their lines when asleep. Also, these same actors would involuntarily fall asleep when saying their lines – which is a condition known as 'Acting Narcolepsy'.

Then there is the 'say it out loud and get someone to read in' technique. This one is particularly handy if you have someone you trust to go through your lines with you. Of course, you should never choose to go through your lines with someone who is a better actor than you, as this results in bitter jealousy and resentment, and you will always end up focusing on that rather than your learning. I recommend asking someone who is not an actor since they will just say the lines and not add their own interpretation. The problem with learning lines with other actors is that they will attempt to give a polished performance, and possibly start criticising your interpretation. Which is not useful at all. As a general rule, your mummy and daddy are the best people to help in the 'reading in' technique – as they will constantly remind you of how good you are and then give you an increase in your pocket money for good behaviour.

You may be fortunate enough to be in a play or musical that has been performed before, which can prove a remarkable tool in your line-learning success. Chances are the musical you are in will have a cast recording, and if you are very lucky the play you are in might be available as an audiobook (or you may find some snippets from it online). Simply purchase the recording, play it on loop and, hey presto, not only have you got someone else saying your lines, but you have someone else showing you *how* to say your lines. Marvellous!

In the past when I've helped actors learn lines, I've always been scolded – as apparently I'm too distracting. But I'm not. I'm just honest. I always say if I think the line is being said wrong, or if I feel jazz hands could be added at certain points. There is nothing wrong with being constructive with your criticism, but always be careful not to overstep the mark. This, I imagine, is a problem that many acting couples have – particularly celebrities. And is the main reason why so many celebrity marriages end in divorce. It is all down to line-learning arguments.

Some actors like the lines to consume them completely, and feel that their performance will only be truly great if the lines seem to come from them organically and internally. So they take it to the next level and literally *eat* their lines. Whilst this approach is extremely dedicated – it is also rather unhealthy and risky. Indeed, there was one company in the early nineties who did this, which resulted in the show being cancelled as the entire cast developed severe constipation. But then it is rather silly eating the text of something as wordy as Tom Stoppard. In fact, there are only a handful of writers to whom you can safely apply this 'eating' method – one of the best being Harold Pinter. His plays are half dialogue, half pauses – so you digest fewer words, with half the calories.

There's going to be a new rule about the length of Pinter pauses. Anything longer than ten seconds incurs a self-indulgence penalty, dear.

As mentioned earlier, some people believe that a good actor doesn't have to bother learning lines – that if they have done their work in rehearsals and studied the script correctly, the lines will go in automatically. This is all well and good if you're playing a supporting character with four lines, but is something of an impossibility if you are playing Hamlet. Unless, of course, you are Kenneth Branagh – in which case you can just say 'de-dum-de-dum-de-dum-de-dum-de-dum', dear.

There is also the question about whether an actor should learn their lines *before* or *after* rehearsals begin. There are arguments for both approaches. Some actors refuse to start work on a script before rehearsals, claiming they aren't being paid to work on it at that point. An actor who learns lines before rehearsals tends to have learnt them with a specific character idea in mind – which can be extremely difficult to change. Many actors think it far easier to learn lines once they've 'put the character on its feet' – so that as they are learning the lines they can visualise where they are standing.

A new method I heard about recently involved a few actors who had recorded their lines onto a device which was then played back to them through a tiny earpiece during the performance. The only problem came when the recording device skipped a few lines, which resulted in them saying their lines in completely the wrong places. Using this method there was a memorable performance of *Oliver!* where Nancy sang a rousing rendition of 'Oom-Pah-Pah' when she was supposed to be singing 'As Long as He Needs Me'. Bless.

Learning lines is hard. But saying them 'out loud' is even harder, dear.

It is very common for an actor to come to rehearsals and proclaim 'I've learnt all my lines!' – only for them to gibber like an idiot as soon as they get to their scene. You see, there is a very large distinction between knowing your lines at home and saying them out loud in the rehearsal room. When on your own all you have to worry about is saying the lines – but when standing in a rehearsal room you have to not only *say* the lines, you have to *act* the lines (which is difficult and should only be attempted by experienced actors). Many people make the mistake of thinking that talking and acting at the same time is easy. It is not. Which is why it is vital that you practise, practise, practise!

If you are unfortunate enough to be in a show where someone doesn't know their lines, it is very tempting to try and help them. Whilst this is very generous, it should be approached with severe caution. An actor's job is to say his own lines, and his own lines *only* – if you start saying someone else's lines not only will it look like you want a bigger role, but also that you are trying to show them how to do their role. It is to be avoided at all costs, even if you feel you are saving the production. The difficulty is that if you help them out every night they will rely on you to prompt them for the rest of the contract – and they will *never* learn their lines. The best thing to do is let them suffer on stage in front of an audience, where they will look like an idiot and be forced to find a way out themselves. They will very quickly realise that they have no other option than to learn their lines. And fast!

Some actors feel the need to go through their lines in public, as they adore the thrill of doing it in front of strangers. Over the years I have spied actors mouthing their lines in coffee houses, buses, public toilets and at international sporting events. Whilst it is not necessarily deemed illegal, it certainly is something that is frowned upon. I have seen entire restaurants cleared of members of the public as an actor gets their script out and talks to himself. It is very unnerving to watch, and makes civilians even more unsure about actors. If you are into this sort of thing I recommend searching the classified section in your local paper for 'acting dogging spots', dear.

Actors – a stage kiss is only meant to last ten seconds. Any longer and it is considered abuse, dear.

Taking Over a Role

The role of an actor in theatre is constantly changing. And a new type of performer that is increasingly prominent is the 'takeover actor'. These kinds of actors are marvellous at going into a long-running show and doing exactly what they are told – by standing in exactly the same places as the actor before them did. They are not employed to be creative or add anything new to the character. They come from a different school of acting – the 'shut up and stand where you are told' method.

A takeover actor will be highly experienced in the art of copying. If they are not, and they resist standing in the same position as the actor before them, they will inevitably miss their light – and consequently do the entire performance in darkness. This is very awkward for the actor, and terribly confusing for the audience.

A takeover actor must also try and say the lines and sing the songs exactly the same way as the person before them did. This reduces the need for musical directors to change tempos unnecessarily. And it also means the other actors won't have to respond in a different way. There is nothing worse than 'throwing' an actor who has been in a show for two years because someone new waltzes in and does something different. This is not the job of the takeover actor. The takeover actor has to make the transition as smoothly as possible, preferably so that the rest of the cast don't even realise that another actor is playing the role. This also avoids the cast having to learn the new actor's name.

In the first few days of a 'takeover cast' rehearsal, the resident director will be very welcoming of your individuality and tell you that you can keep it 'fresh' by bringing in new ideas. This is a lie. It simply isn't possible in terms of time and money to have every new cast member doing something different. Look at all the long-running musicals in the West End. They have only lasted because of the fine, talented and inspirational performers who came in and did exactly what the person before them was doing.

The Threats of Actors

If you feel your individual disciplines of acting, singing and dancing are strong, you may feel ready to take it to the next stage. This is where you could become a 'triple-threat actor'! Triple-threat actors are a new species of actor that, until recently, never used to exist, but due to genetic engineering, cross-breeding and contaminated water, these super-performing machines are no longer a thing of dreams.

In the industry there was a belief that these new breed of 'threat' actors were being mass-produced by a sweatshop factory in Southern America, but recently this was disproved when a label on Summer Strallen was discovered saying 'Made in China'.

Different Types of Threat

No threat – The cast of *Hollyoaks*.

Single threat – An actor who can act, sing or dance. But not at the same time.

Double threat – An actor who can act, sing or dance whilst doing a ball-change.

Triple threat – An actor who can sing, act and dance all to a high level – and, where required, at the same time.

Quadruple threat – An actor who can sing, act, dance and play an instrument. (Playing random notes on the recorder does not count.)

Quintuple threat – An actor who can sing, act, dance, play instruments and juggle.

Sextuple threat – An actor who can sing, act, dance, play instruments, juggle and ride a horse.

Septuple threat – An actor who can sing, act, dance, play instruments, juggle, ride a horse and is good at poaching an egg. And Sheridan Smith.

Octuple threat – Kevin Spacey. And his dog. At 4 a.m. in the morning.

Any actors who consider themselves above a quintuple threat are treated with caution – as these people tend to spontaneously combust due to talent overload. My advice to these kinds of performers is to go and work in admin. It's a lot safer.

A word of warning: Never talk about what level of threat you think you are. This can cause embarrassment, particularly if other people disagree with your assessment. In this industry it is much better to be self-deprecating. If others want to flatter you, let them. Never flatter yourself. Unless you are *really* good. In which case, go for it.

I am currently lobbying Spotlight to allocate a 'threat' status option in the actor's 'skills' section. This will allow your agent to input what threat of an actor you are – and save lots of precious audition time and money. For example, if I need sixteen quintuple-threat actors who can play the didgeridoo, this simple tool will save my casting director years of searching.

It's a sad truth, but to succeed in the business these days you need to be highly skilled in all areas. It's just like if you are an IT expert, being proficient on Excel is not enough – you also have to be skilled in Word, Outlook, PowerPoint and PornHider – and because there are so many actors out there each discipline has to be finely honed. However, being a multiskilled performer also has its disadvantages – as you can be considered a 'jack-of-all-trades-master-of-none'.

If you are lucky enough to have floppy hair, a posh voice, and some lovely brogues then your first job will be at the RSC. But if, at the beginning of your career, you do a musical, then a play, then a cabaret, then a cruise ship, then a physical-theatre piece, then back to an acting piece – your CV looks confusing as it doesn't look like you specialise in one type of performance. Which is the frustrating thing – because you can do them all! So, I suggest being clever with your CV, and only putting jobs on there that sell you as the type of actor you want to be. If you want to be a serious actor, just put plays and TV credits on. This makes it far more likely that a casting director will take you seriously. If you have a CV that's full of all different disciplines, a casting director and director won't know what to do with you. In one respect you are more cast-able when just leaving drama school – as you are a blank canvas. For example, if you have been working professionally for years and have only theatre credits on your CV, it's very unlikely a TV casting director will call you in. So decide what kind of actor you are. However, by saying this I don't mean you should turn all work down. Work leads to work, and contacts lead to contacts – but just be conscious of what kind of actor you will be perceived as.

We recently auditioned a girl who said she was a triple threat. The only thing threatening about her was the size of her teeth, dear.

To Be a Leading Actor, or Not to Be a Leading Actor – That is the Question

As mentioned earlier, deciding what kind of roles you want to play is very important. Many actors will only accept 'leading roles' so that they continue being known as a 'leading actor', whilst other actors are happy to get two solo lines in an entire show. It all depends what kind of an actor you see yourself as.

Many people argue that there are no leading actors, that in fact the company as a *whole* are the leading actors. Whilst this is a very nice, idealistic vision of theatre, it is sadly not how it works. Every show has a lead, a supporting actor and an ensemble. Many times it is the lead who the audience are going to watch – and you will notice that even if a show is supposed to be an 'ensemble' piece, the lead's name and photo will be on all the marketing and PR material. So, of course, they are then 'looked on' as being the leads.

Different Types of Actors

A **leading actor** will have the most lines and usually the play/show will be based around their character. As a rule they will have been cast before anyone else is auditioned – just so that everyone 'works' around them. Although they are playing the most significant role in the show, they may not be the best-qualified person to do it. But they will have excellent 'bums on seats' value – making them hugely attractive to production companies and investors.

A **supporting actor** will have quite a few lines, but substantially less than the lead. They will usually be in a couple of scenes, and help move the story along. A supporting actor will have some nice TV credits and/or some lovely theatre roles on their CV. These actors will have slight 'bums on seats' value – and will be vaguely recognisable from *Heartbeat*.

An **ensemble actor** will be one of the most talented in the company. They will not only be playing a small role in the show, but will be understudying the leading actors. They will also be integral in all the dance numbers, and their singing voices will be what makes the numbers sound so wonderful. They will be singing all the difficult harmony lines, and dancing the hardest choreography. They will also be on the least amount of money – which is why I can always afford more of them.

The Actors' Alphabet

Over the years, my PA and I have come up with an alphabet to classify all the different types of actors. I find this particularly helpful when writing notes during auditions. What kind of actor are you, dear?

Actor – Someone who can remember their lines in the correct order.

Bactor – A bad actor.

Craptor – A really bad actor.

Divactor – A diva.

Ector – An eccentric actor.

Factor – An actor who has been on *The X Factor*.

Gintor – A ginger actor.

Hamster – A furry little animal.

Ictor – An actor who can do a good impression of a dinosaur.

Jactor – A jack of all trades, master of none.

Kacktor – An actor who has a tendency to kack his pants.

Lactor – A large actor.

Mactor – A musical-theatre actor. Or an actor who only works in shows produced by Cameron Mackintosh.

Nactor – A Northern actor.

Octor – An old actor.

Pactor – A posh actor.

Quactor – A quirky actor.

Ractor – An RSC actor.

Sactor – A Scottish actor.

Tractor – An actor who can drive farming equipment.

Uctor – An actor from Uttoxeter.

Vactor – An actor who can drive a van (good for TIE tours).

Wactor – A Welsh actor.

X-actor – An actor who has given up.

Yactor – A youthful actor.

Zactor – A Z-list celeb actor.

The Actors' Alphabet in Action

'We auditioned a nactor yesterday who used to be a ractor, but now sadly he's just a craptor.'

'The problem with factors are they act like divactors, but are in actual fact zactors.'

'That mactor is really very good. And he's a tractor. I do hope he's not a bactor.'

That old saying 'There are no small parts only small actors' is a complete lie. Of course there are small parts. I pay them a lot less, dear.

Animal Actors

There are many plays and films that require animal actors. And, whilst many modern films use CGI effects, in theatre particularly there has always been a demand for *real* animals. For example, both *Annie* and *The Wizard of Oz* require dogs. I hear that Andrew Lloyd Webber has always planned to do a production of *Cats* with a real feline cast. It really sounds quite marvellous. In fact, I understand Lloyd Webber is getting an extension on his conservatory at Sydmonton so he can house and train them all himself. But then Andrew always did love being surrounded by pussies. Bless.

Animal actors have to be trained properly, and require just as much dedication and talent as a normal human actor. There are, however, many differences between a human and animal actor – the most obvious being their lack of toilet etiquette and abundance of hair. But, as a general rule, it is very easy to tell the difference between animals and humans on stage, unless, of course, the human is Brian Blessed.

Animal actors and performers have become even more popular recently due to Pudsey the dog winning *Britain's Got Talent*. That amazing canine proved that many people consider a talented dog to be far more entertaining than a talented human. Which only goes to show why so many dogs have had excellent West End careers.

One of the most well-known sayings in the entertainment business is 'Don't work with animals or children.' I personally don't agree with this – and have been pleasantly surprised at just how willing and adaptable an animal can be. In fact, I know many animal actors who are far better than human actors. They are certainly more obedient for starters. A dear director friend of mine is currently training human actors to be more like animal actors by putting them on a lead and making them fetch sticks in the rehearsal room. It really sounds intriguing. And is having a profound effect on the actor playing King Lear.

There is often a lot of bitterness between animal and human performers – mostly because the animals get more money. This is for various reasons, one of the main ones being we have to pay not only the animal but also their trainer. On top of that, animal actors are very demanding, and require their dressing room to be filled with a new supply of Pedigree Chum every day. Of course, we have to do this, because unlike human actors, the dogs actually bite back. There are also some very well-known human actors who do this. But for legal reasons I cannot name them.

Because of the new popularity in animal actors there are now many drama institutions who specialise in this field – and, rather like schools for human actors, they offer one-, two- and three-year courses.

The best animal drama schools are listed below:

RADA – Royal Academy of Dog Art.

LAMDA – London Academy of Mutated Dog Actors (crossbreeds).

RCSSD – Royal Central School of Snakes and Drama.

ArtsEd – Specialises in musical-theatre animals.

LIPA – Liverpool Institute of Performing Animals.

ALRA – Academy of Live and Rare-Breed Animals.

Drama Centre London – Specialises in training tough/ arrogant animals.

The Poor School – For animal actors who can't afford the other schools.

A quick plea: if you are an animal actor that can swim, please get in touch. I am desperately searching for a whale that can sing, dance, and has puppetry skills for my upcoming musical production of *Free Willy*.

Naming your baby 'The National Theatre' is very committed, but does not guarantee success, dear.

Stagecraft

Stagecraft is something of a dying tradition. There used to be a time when every actor knew how to behave on stage, and was only too aware of essential techniques that would aid their performance. Today, however, many young actors even get confused as to where the front and back of the stage is. They have no idea how to 'find their light' and get terrified about working without radio mics. It really is rather depressing.

I remember a time when actors used to rehearse quickly, perform eagerly and drink heavily. There was no time for sitting in circles discussing the script for weeks on end before actors got on their feet. Rehearsals were speedy, and every minute was valuable. And as well as rehearsing in the day, actors performed shows in the evening. I am, of course, referring to the old repertory system.

These old rep theatres, and their marvellous way of working, is hugely missed by actors and audiences alike. The very nature of having the same actors playing a variety of shows, and the theatre 'community' that was created, commanded a supportive and faithful audience, who would watch every show. And, indeed, the actors were also faithful – they would go back year after year to work on different plays in roles that would challenge and stretch them. Young people were forced to play old people, old women were forced to play schoolchildren, and old men were forced to play with any young person they could find. It was a glorious time of creation.

Rep theatre also used to be the old 'training ground' for actors. Of course, actors still went to drama school, but they really learnt their craft on the job. I suppose it could be said that rep theatres provided the first artistic 'apprenticeships' – where actors would have the opportunity to play different roles, help backstage, make props, stage manage, and learn four or five different plays simultaneously. It really was the best learning experience for all involved, allowing actors to experience and work in every aspect of theatre. These days you are either an actor, crew member, wardrobe assistant, techie or front-of-house worker – you are rarely allowed to practise more than one of these disciplines. Rep theatre allowed you to be all of them, creating fully rounded actors who appreciated and understood all areas of theatre.

Now, sadly, there are only a couple of theatres that operate using a rep system. And whenever I go into one I am reminded of how wonderful and vital they are. I have always thought that a musical-theatre rep would be rather fun – where different musicals are performed on alternating weeks with the same cast. It would just be difficult convincing Elaine Paige and Michael Ball to do all of that for Equity minimum though, dear.

In many ways, the luxury of time can be a creativity killer. Although it allows themes and subtext to be explored completely, there is only so much subtext you can find in *Beauty and the Beast*. Working to a tight deadline and feeling the pressure of opening night is marvellous – it instils an essential urgency in the rehearsal room. And that can be hugely rewarding. It forces actors to follow their gut and be instinctive about their characters without sitting back and analysing what and why they are doing things. In fact, most actors like nothing more than standing up with the script on day one of rehearsals and simply going for it.

Having a few stagecraft secrets is very useful. Particularly when playing to empty houses, or working with actors who can't walk or talk properly. They are empowering little tips that help you get all the focus, and ensure that the audience is always aware of you whenever you are on stage.

Walking On Stage and Back Acting

Always walk on stage using your upstage leg. This means your whole body will be on show to the audience. If you make your first entrance with your downstage leg, you risk the chance of the audience firstly seeing your back. This is only useful if you are technically experienced in 'back acting'.

Back acting is something which has been passed down to actors for generations. It is only suitable for certain actors, those that are prepared to have their face away from the audience for long periods of time.

Actors who have big backs or distinctive shoulder blades are naturally gifted in the art of back acting. It is the clever discipline of being able to convey emotion through the dramatic use of your back. One of the joys of back acting is not being able to see the front of the actor, allowing the audience to be more creative as they imagine what the actor's face is doing. I tried to convince Nicky Hytner to host a 'Back Acting' season at the National for years (a *Hamlet* acted entirely from the back would be thrilling), but Nicky stopped returning my calls. How rude. (Fingers crossed for Rufus Norris.)

Here are some basic guidelines in the sacred art of back acting: If you lift your shoulders you appear stressed; if you stick your neck up you appear inquisitive; and if you tilt your head to one side you appear to have a deformity. There are also other more challenging positions like shaking your back from side to side (when miming doing the hula hoop) and sticking your shoulder blades out (when playing vampires) – but these should be approached with caution.

Words, Words, Words

If you have words in your script that repeat, always try and make them sound different, as it makes them far more interesting to listen to. Unless, of course, you decide your character wouldn't do that. In which case you can say them all the same. Which makes this point invalid. So please disregard it.

The Fourth Wall

The 'fourth wall' is an imaginary wall at the front of the stage that allows the audience to look in on the action of the show. It is a term that is used widely by directors and drama tutors as it gives the impression they know what they're talking about. But, in truth, they rarely do.

Many actors, particularly when making their stage debut, get very confused about the fourth wall – and often forget that it isn't real. This can be very distressing, particularly when actors lean on it and fall onto an unsuspecting old dear sitting in the front row. Accidents like this ruin the play completely, and make everyone more than aware that the fourth wall doesn't exist.

The fourth wall was invented by a set designer who was high on amphetamines in the sixties as a result of a difficult problem he was having with the director. The director was insisting on a set with four walls, so that the actors were boxed into a real house, making it totally naturalistic. Of course, whilst this was all well and good, it meant that the audience would only be able to see a brick wall. The director argued that they'd still be able to *hear* the action inside – transforming the audience into a community of 'neighbours listening in'. So the set designer was faced with a problem. Although he disagreed with the director, he was also being paid by the director. So, after much coffee and speed, he decided the best thing to do was create an 'invisible' wall. It was a genius idea as it was far more creative than a proper wall, and allowed the audience and actors to imagine whatever kind of wall they wanted. Ultimately, the director got his wall, the actors got their audience, and the audience got more than a pile of bricks. And it went down a treat! Hence the birth of the fourth wall.

Nowadays the fourth wall is constantly used in productions, but is often taken for granted. This is dangerous – and causes actors to forget about it – particularly when they start 'eyeing up' cuties in the first few rows. You must always fight this tendency and keep up the pretence that the wall is there. However, always remember that this does not mean you can throw things at it, hang things on it, lean on it or expect it to make a noise when you tap it. It isn't real, dear!

Eyes On the Floor

Unless you are making a very brave character choice there really is no need to spend your entire performance staring at the floor. For one thing, it makes you appear nervous, and secondly, it stops the audience seeing your face and connecting with you. Whilst I understand that it may be very comforting staring at the floor – particularly if you're wearing some nice costume shoes – it is infuriating to watch. You will generally find that audience members don't like paying £50 to stare at an actor's bald patch.

If the reason you stare at the floor is because you are actually scared of seeing the audience, there are far better options. One of them is to become a plumber. Another is to wear some wrong-strength contact lenses – making everything blurry. This will prevent you from seeing any of the audience and, as a bonus, will also stop you seeing your fellow actors (which is particularly useful if you are working with some uglies).

....

To be a successful actor you have to do more than simply shout. You have to shout in the right direction.

....

How to Sound Like a Proper Actor

After you have been in the business for a few minutes you will quickly realise that there is a particular way that actors speak. As well as talking about previous shows they've been in, actors like to discuss anything that is relevant in the acting world, and on a continual basis. This is at once wonderfully, ridiculously passionate, and also draining. Being surrounded by actors all the time makes you pick up certain mannerisms.

Below is a list of useful phrases that you will recognise instantly. If you want to sound like a professional actor you should start using these examples as soon as you can. After all, to be a professional actor, you must sound like a professional actor, dear.

Common Things That Musical-theatre Performers Say

'What's your range?'
'I did the original cast recording.'
'Should I sing this in my head or chest voice?'
'Anyone got a Vocalzone?'
'My throat hurts.'
'I don't feel very open today.'
'What a rubbish warm-up.'
'I'm more of a singer than an actor.'
'Are you working at the moment?
'Are you auditioning for anything at the moment?'
'I got a recall!'
'Can I have a poster?'
'Sorry, I can't, I have rehearsal.'

'What's our call time?'
'I'm not paid enough to sing that note.'
'Could we transpose it?'
'My mic doesn't fit properly.'
'What's my harmony again?'
'Do I get a solo line?'
'Was I pitchy?'
'Idina told me she liked me.'
'I can't find my note.'
'Can I belt that bit?'
'Sorry. I left my talent at home today.'
'I feel so blessed to be in this show.'
'You're like my family.'
'Hold on a minute, I've just got to siren.'
'It's not dirt… it's just mic tape.'
'Is your agent in tonight?'

Common Things That Actors Say

'I'm playing the lead.'
'No eye contact, please.'
'I'm more of an actor than a singer.'
'I'm not the lead, but I'm the next most important part.'
'Are you working at the moment?
'I got a recall for that.'
'I was in the original production.'
'I know her.'
'I slept with her.'
'I slept with her twice.'

'I love Shakespeare.'
'I'm getting into character.'
'That show went really well.'
'Are you auditioning for anything at the moment?'
'When do we need to be off-book?'
'Do I exit stage-left or stage-right?'
'Can I be at centre-stage at this point?'
'Can you hear me back there?'
'Who's your agent?'
'Is it tea break yet?'
'Stop upstaging me.'
'I don't want to be Equity deputy.'
'I definitely want to be Equity deputy.'
'What does that word mean?'
'I don't want to do a pre-set at the half.'
'Apparently this might be transferring.'
'I used to be with your agent.'
'Did you get seen for that?'
'Are you going to do it like that on the night?'
'Did your agent send you flowers?'
'Anyone got a spare highlighter?'

Common Things That Stage Management Say

'Don't touch the props. Leave the props alone.'
'Actors – get off the stage.'
'Going black on stage.'
'Tabs in.'
'Get out of the way, please.'

'Get out of the way NOW.'
'Get out of the way NOW otherwise we will squash you.'
'Do you like my new black top?'
'Shhhhhhhh!'
'No talking backstage.'
'Where are your blacks?'
'Miss_____ or Mr _____ – you are *off*!'

Common Things That Directors Say

'Act better.'
'What's your motivation?'
'Get off stage quicker.'
'Have you even read the script?'
'When are you going to be off-book, love?'
'I thought that was a great run. But it still needs
a lot of work.'
'It's got to look organic.'
'Don't worry – this readthrough is not an audition.'
'What is your objective in this scene?'
'Faster and funnier, please.'
'Forget about the Method – just say the bloody lines.'
'Remember your blocking.'
'I did not tell you to do that.'
'Remember – this is a play, not a panto.'
'Remember – this is a play, not a musical.'
'Ibsen was not born in Essex, love.'
'It's in great shape.'
'See you at the tech.'

The Technical Rehearsal

I often hear actors complaining about a particularly horrific time they spend in the theatre. It is a time when the director ignores them, the musical director is more concerned about the band and his baton, and the lighting and sound designers get all the praise. It is a time when actors are sadly reminded that they are merely paid to stand in the right lights, speak in the right places, and look nice. It's a sad day, an awakening, a time when actors wish that they were getting paid as much as the person who found the sound effects. And a time when everyone realises that they've put on weight since the wardrobe mistress measured them four weeks ago. Yes, that's right – it is the technical rehearsal. Aka 'the Tech'!

Technical rehearsals are invariably long, tedious, awkward and violent days. They involve lots of standing around, waiting in the wings, awkward fist fights and missed tea breaks. It is a trying time when tempers are high, and actors leave the business to drive buses. Only the other day I was travelling to Swiss Cottage and discovered my bus was being driven by Serena McKellen. He was very helpful when I had Oyster card issues, dear.

The tech usually occurs on the first day you arrive at the theatre. Whether you are opening a national tour, a show in the West End, or a TIE version of *Les Liaisons Dangereuses*, this first day in the venue can be very exciting indeed.

It is lovely visiting your new theatre for the first time – usually you will see your show poster outside the building, which always makes actors feel warm inside. But on closer inspection many actors see that their name or photo isn't on the poster – it's only the director, MD, choreographer, lighting designer, sound designer, set designer and local bin man. This is where actors realise that they took the wrong course at drama school – and should have done the three-year technical-theatre course instead.

Upon entering a new theatre you will be greeted by the stage-door keeper. These people are very important – and know the theatre inside out. Many of them are undercover spies for MI5, and all of them are karate champions. It is a well-guarded secret that to become a fully qualified stage-door keeper you have to do a five-year course at Oxford University. Stage-door keepers can become your loyal friend, or your worst enemy. There is a legend that the stage-door keeper at the Theatre Royal, Drury Lane is actually Lord Lucan.

Dressing Rooms

After being accepted by Lord Lucan you will be allowed to your dressing room. Many actors refer to their dressing room as 'home'. It is not. You do not pay the mortgage. And you do not pay rent. The only people who are allowed to call it 'home' are the theatre rats. And Simon Russell Beale. I'm sure his permanent place of residence is the National Theatre. He always seems to be hanging around there anyway, dear.

Unless you are the star of the show you will invariably be sharing your dressing room. This is not a bad thing if you like your fellow cast members – but can prove something of a problem if you are sitting next to a 'sweaty Betty'. Every cast has a sweaty Betty – and, like the company idiot, if you don't know who this person is, then the likelihood is that it's you. The sweaty Betty of the cast tends to smell of old bacon and has a habit of eating Scampi Fries all the way through the interval.

One of the most important things to do when getting into a new theatre is finding where the tea and coffee is. Usually such items are kept in the green room – but sometimes they're hidden so the actors can't find them. This never goes down well, particularly first thing in the morning. I remember an actor in 1985 getting so angry about the lack of coffee in a particular theatre that he vowed to make a mockery of the show and be as 'over the top' as possible. Luckily for Antony Sher he's made a successful career out of this ever since.

Actors – the further away your dressing room is from the stage, the less important you are.

The Sound Check

A vital element of any musical's tech is the sound check. Actors love sound checks. They suddenly feel very important as everyone is forced to listen to them. It's their moment to shine, and show off their marvellous voice whilst everyone else in the theatre is forced to endure the agonising torture of their raised soft palate. But then, of course, the actor goes on stage and freezes. What should an actor say at the sound check? They have just had their radio microphones fitted, and are required to simply talk on stage. It really should be something actors are very good at, but the moment they're standing alone on that stage, with the rest of the cast and creative team watching and listening – invariably all they know how to say is 'One, two, one, two.' I often suggest to actors that they recite some lines from the show, but this is only the technical rehearsal and most actors don't know their lines by then. That is what the preview period is for, dear.

I remember one actor in Scarborough who decided to recite the whole of his CV during the sound check. He was talking for about fifteen minutes. Which is remarkable considering all he'd done was a summer season at Frinton-on-Sea.

At the back of the auditorium you will usually see a tall shadowy figure slumped around a desk, frequently cursing, and calling actors 'plebs'. This isn't a Tory MP – it's the sound technician. This is the person who controls the microphone levels, sound effects and pre-recorded music. They are usually very nice people, but can be rather smelly. I recently approached Lynx and challenged them to try and combat the body odour of one very pungent sound technician. But they said the 'Lynx effect' doesn't apply to people working backstage in a theatre.

It is advisable to be very friendly with the sound technician. If they don't like you, they have the ultimate power and will stop your voice being heard. I know lots of people who complain about the use of radio microphones these days and say, 'But surely actors can project.' I have seen lots of actors project over the years – but most of the time it's after eight pints and involves vomit, dear.

Costumes and Set

The tech also includes the excitement of trying on your costume. This is where you regret eating all of my HobNobs during rehearsals. A costume which was designed to make you look slim and slender now makes you look like you're the lead in *Russell Grant: The Musical*. It's not all bad though – this is what the technical rehearsal is for. You simply ask your dresser to force a very tight corset, or length of cling film, around your waist, and once again you are reduced to a size 8. If the actors are very excited they will sometimes offer 'extra services' to the costume designer in exchange for a better frock, and the designer will disappear into the actor's dressing room for a few minutes. If a designer is very lucky they may get the chance to visit every dressing room in the theatre.

Then there is the joy seeing the set for the first time. Actors always giggle and laugh hysterically the moment they see it. If the designer is around, the actors gravitate towards him or her, and compliment them on their success.

For the directors, the success of the set is also hugely important – as it can take the focus off the bad acting, and fool the audience into thinking the show is a lot better than it actually is.

Before the full technical rehearsal begins the director and designer will sometimes demand a 'costume show' on stage. This is where the actors get to parade around the stage and imagine they are all models. Always remember at this point to wear exactly what the designer has told you to wear. If you decide you want to wear your own costume that you've recently purchased from Primark, only do this after week two of the run – when the designer is in Russia working on the tour of *La Cage aux Folles*, dear.

Most of the time the 'sitzprobe' (where actors sing with the band for the first time) will already have happened – but when actors hear the band, see the set and wear the costumes simultaneously they get overexcited, and end up in a dribbling heap downstage-right. This condition is very well known in the industry – and many premature actors suffer from it. The 'showgasm' is something which can affect actors of every age and experience. Apparently Patrick Stewart had a 'showgasm' when he first saw the set of *Macbeth* – and ended up 'showgasming' all over the three witches.

The Tea Break

After the sound check and the costume show you may be lucky and get a fifteen-minute tea break. The tea break is a very important time – as it allows the actors to congregate in the green room or stare at themselves in their dressing-room mirrors. 'Staring at yourself in the dressing-room mirror' is an ancient theatrical tradition that has been passed down since Laurence Olivier invented drama in the 1960s.

As the first tech session starts, actors are reminded to stay calm and breathe deeply. Sometimes actors are lucky and will have a marvellous company manager who will hand out Valium which has been kindly provided by Equity. If Valium is not available, actors will use Lemsip, vodka, beer, or simply suck on an unhealthy number of Vocalzones, dear.

The length of a tech can vary hugely. It all depends on the size, scale and challenges of the show. If you are doing a 'mid-scale tour', the tech will last two days, if you are doing a panto in Margate the tech will last two hours, and if you are doing a show at the RSC the tech will last a year. So it is vital you keep your energy levels up, and let your loved ones know you will not be contactable for the foreseeable future.

It is not uncommon that during the technical rehearsal actors get shocked at the sound of their own voices. They hear themselves amplified around the stage and realise that they actually sound dreadful. This is awkward as the director has known this for weeks. In cases where the actors get anxious as a result of this I remind them to 'think of the money'. Then I remember that they are on Equity minimum and tell them to think of England.

Technical rehearsals can even change an entire performance. When on stage you may realise that the lighting designer has decided to light the scene entirely differently to how you have rehearsed it – meaning you have to change where you stand and talk. This will teach you for not sleeping with them the night before.

If all else fails, and actors feel they cannot cope with the strains and stresses of the technical rehearsal, I suggest they go back to RADA for their new three-year course: 'How to Survive a Technical Rehearsal'.

After you have successfully completed the tech there is only one thing to do: reward yourself by going to the pub and getting savagely sloshed. Unless, of course, the technical rehearsal finishes an hour before your first show (which it frequently does). In which case, break a leg! You're going to need it, dear.

Traditions and Superstitions

The Green Room

The green room is the place where actors and stage management sit, bitch and drink. It is a place of sanctity that offers a change of scenery from the stage and dressing rooms. Of course, most green rooms carry a 'public health warning' as they are never cleaned. But they are very important places and usually have a TV, microwave and kettle. Indeed, some green rooms even have a selection of magazines to keep people occupied. Magazines that comprise mostly of porn. Which is a sure way of keeping actors quiet during the interval.

There are many thoughts and theories about where the term 'green room' originated, but here is my favourite. In Restoration theatre – in the late seventeenth century – costumes were elaborate and very expensive. And they were never washed. So actors had to be extremely diligent in keeping their costumes clean. This is why Restoration plays are traditionally performed in specific poses and stances – with the arms outstretched and legs apart – so that costumes do not touch and rub, and get dirty. However, theatres are filthy places, and the very nature of performing in them resulted in costumes and actors getting dirty and sweaty. The task of keeping costumes clean was particularly difficult when a character was expected to 'die' on stage. The thought of having an elaborate 'writhing around on the floor death' used to terrify Restoration actors as it was a sure way of getting their costumes dirty. This is where the green room came in. The green room was used to store a lot of green material (rather like the baize on a snooker table) – and at the precise moment an actor had to die, someone would run on stage and lay down a piece of this material so the death could happen without the costume getting filthy. Because lots of these strips of green material were left in a room near the stage it became known as the 'green room'.

The other reason it is called the green room is because if you are an actor who spends a lot of time in there you will be 'green with envy' that you aren't spending more time on stage playing a bigger part, dear.

No Whistling On Stage

You should avoid whistling on stage – or indeed offstage – for fear of things being dropped on your head. This dates back to when the people who used to build sets and help with rigging were hired from ships and boats in port. And as anyone who has worked backstage will know, crew members delight in showing off all the different knots they know – knots which were passed down and learnt from sailors.

On ships, the sailors would communicate by whistling certain calls and tunes which meant particular things (like 'drop the sail') – and this is how sailors also communicated in theatres. So if an actor whistled on stage he could accidentally be instructing a sailor/crew member to drop in a piece of scenery.

However, there are times when this tradition can be rather useful – particularly if you are understudying someone and fancy a go at the role. Simply do a lot of whistling at the appropriate moment and hope that a sailor drops a nice bit of heavy scenery onto their head. Naughty, dear.

Macbeth

The play *Macbeth* is apparently cursed, and if anyone says the name aloud in a theatre it is thought to bring bad luck. To get around this, people call it 'The Scottish Play'.

It is cursed because apparently the witches' spells are *actual* spells that Shakespeare copied down and used in the play. I find this rather hard to believe, and haven't seen any actual evidence – unless, of course, the spell is to make the actors playing Macbeth and Lady Macbeth have an affair. In which case the spell definitely works, dear.

Another reason for this superstition is that *Macbeth* contains more sword fights than any other Shakespearean play – so there is more chance of an accident. It is also believed that shortly after the first production of the play, the actor playing Macbeth died. I have subsequently seen many actors playing Macbeth who looked like they were dying on stage night after night. Bless them.

Traditionally, if an actor says 'Macbeth' in a theatre they have to leave the building, do a 10K run, down two pints of cider, sing 'The Circle of Life' backwards, rub a copy of the *Complete Works of Shakespeare* all over their naughty region, and defecate on a recently graduated drama student.

Pantomime Superstitions

In a pantomime it is considered bad luck to perform the whole piece without an audience – which means that it should never be fully performed before opening night. This can be something of a problem during dress rehearsals – when it is vital to do a full run. The way superstitious directors get around this is by not allowing the actors to say the final two lines of the show (which are traditionally rhyming couplets) until the opening night. This is fine if those two lines are easy, but a bloody nightmare if they're not.

There is also the belief that the 'good' characters (Fairy Godmother/Genie) should only enter stage-right, and the 'bad' characters (Abanazar/King Rat) should enter stage-left. This is because in old theatres the baddie would make their first entrance rising from a trapdoor that was always on the left side of the stage. Also, in folklore, the 'good' side is always the right side – which explains why Ant is always on the left, and Dec is on the right, dear.

The Dress Rehearsal

There is a silly superstition that if you have a bad dress rehearsal you will have an excellent opening night. I understand the idea – that if the dress is a complete failure then nerves, energy and a desire to make it work will empower you to have a marvellous first show. Personally, though, I much prefer it if the dress rehearsal is a success. For one thing there is usually a photographer present, taking photos for front-of-house and marketing purposes – and we don't want bad photos going front-of-house, otherwise what will the box-office staff think? And secondly, I often invite industry friends to see the dress rehearsal – or 'open dress' as it is known – alongside colleagues, friends and theatre staff. It is a marvellous way of getting a true audience reaction – which is invaluable for the actors. It also provides the perfect opportunity for me to show off in front of all my friends, dear.

'Break a Leg'

The term 'break a leg' is said to actors so that people can avoid saying 'good luck' (which is considered bad luck).

The term itself refers to bowing, because when you bow you bend at the knees and 'break' the line of your leg. Hence 'break a leg' means 'take a bow'.

It also refers to when audience members used to throw money onto the stage during the curtain call – causing actors to break the line of their leg by kneeling to pick up the money. I always think it such a shame that this tradition no longer happens – as most actors I know love getting on their knees for money.

It is also bad luck for actors to bow if they feel they haven't performed well and don't 'deserve' it. However, if this rule was followed properly there would be a lot of actors out there who would never bow at all. You know who you are...

THE INTERVAL

Please remember – the interval is not the intercourse, dear.

And here we are, at the interval.

The interval is a marvellous time. A time when ice cream is consumed, bladders are emptied and alcohol is funnelled into welcoming livers. It is a time when couples argue about whether they remembered to record *Corrie*, and drama students take bets on which of the dancers they will snog in the pub afterwards.

It is also the time when eager, excitable, and educated folk enjoy perusing the theatre programme. Generally, theatre programmes offer a little bit of interesting information about the show, interspersed with lots of adverts and pointless information that has nothing to do with anything whatsoever. However, they always include little photos of the actors so that you can spend the rest of the evening figuring out who is playing which part.

If you are unable to read you have the option of spending approximately £10 on a souvenir brochure. These large folders of fun contain lots of big, colourful photos of the actors and creative team acting, rehearsing and laughing at the fact that people pay so much for this silly bit of merchandise.

There now follows some interval entertainment for you to read at your leisure, dear.

Disclaimer: I must state, to protect myself and my family, that this secret was shared with me one evening whilst I was drinking a ludicrous amount of Dom. It is not a factual story and, in truth, was entirely made up. Any well-known personalities mentioned in this passage are mentioned merely for a bit of fun. It is not to be taken seriously. (Hopefully this will prevent me from being taken to court for libel.) All that being said – the story made me laugh. So I had to share it.

The Theatre Mafia

There is a legend about London's organised crime ring that, until now, has not been voiced. It fills me with fear and trepidation to share these findings – but I feel now the time is right.

London's Mafia has always been well-guarded. Over the years, getting involved and surviving has always been a deadly business. If you found yourself dealing with them, or crossing them in any way, then you were lucky to survive. It is a family, a unit, and one of the most powerful untouched organisations working in the world today.

Over the last forty years, the Mafia has been working under a different territory – using different tactics and masquerading as something you would never imagine. They have been meticulous in the way they have developed, and are enshrined in an inner circle of mystery and suspicion.

In the late sixties, London's organised crime ring changed. Everyone predicted something big was going to happen when the Kray Twins went down. It was a scary time – people had to keep their heads low until they knew what was going on. And what was going on was very smart indeed.

At the end of 1969, a man of huge charisma and passion decided it was time to use his considerable influence and powers of persuasion to make a change in London. Since his childhood he knew that he needed to control the capital. He had a master plan, a stroke of genius. Something that would allow him to control areas of the city bit by bit, without anyone having the faintest idea. He was the most unlikely candidate for the job – cleverly posing as an outsider. He was an underdog, a fighter, a rebel with a cause. And a theatrical genius.

He was Cameron Mackintosh.

On money which he raised from various bank jobs, Mackintosh began funding small-scale theatre tours. It was a cunning way to start. He hung around with up-and-coming celebrities who would become his friends. These celebs would eventually vouch for him, support him, and become part of his Mafia family. Once word spread of this eager, young and charismatic man, people started to take notice. His powerful connections increased, and his name was whispered in all the right places – underground stations and Soho brothels.

It was in the early seventies that his slow bid to run London really started to develop. He produced a few short musicals, some of which were not successful – but this didn't matter. It was just a ruse so he had a legitimate business to hide his underworld finances. It was all going very well. His family and criminal racket were starting to take over areas of London by running theatres. This allowed him to form close partnerships with powerful entertainment bosses, young eager actors and local prostitutes. His influence was growing.

However, in the years that followed a rival 'Boss' came onto the scene – Andrew Lloyd Webber. Lloyd Webber had heard of Mackintosh – and was using the same theatrical tactics to take over London's crime world. Lloyd Webber became very well known in the late sixties due to the popular success of *Joseph and his Amazing Technicolor Dreamcoat* (a musical about a boy who takes over the family business with the use of a brightly coloured anorak). The show was a huge success – and with his 'silent but deadly' henchman Tim Rice, Lloyd Webber began making his mark.

But Lloyd Webber's success didn't go down well with Mackintosh – and after minutes of fury and worry he decided the best thing was to combine powers. So after a rather messy fist fight in The Windmill Club – the two decided to become one – heralding the birth of the UK's biggest ever crime ring: The Really Useful Mackintosh.

The aim was simple. Have a succession of hit musicals, become close with London's elite, own theatres throughout London, and have an army of superhuman actors. Owning the venues was the main objective, because it gave criminal gangs and fellow Mafia bosses the perfect place to hide. But the biggest advantage of all was having London actors at their beck and call. Actors who were prepared to do anything. Actors who would be their army.

But, of course, this army needed training. It was no good having an army of pretty dancers who could only pirouette and ball-change in front of rival gangs. No. These actors had to be specially trained, and equipped with survival skills and dirty fighting tactics. They had to be quick-witted and violent. They had to be threatening to opponents. They had to be real *triple threats*. And what better place for them to be trained than at drama school. The top London schools were now being financed by Lloyd Webber and Mackintosh – and this was the reason why.

Obviously the staff at these schools were involved (the name Mackintosh only had to be mentioned and they wept with fear), and because the students were eager to please it was the perfect cover. These actors would be skilled performers; they would sing, dance, act... and kill. That is exactly the purpose of stage-combat classes. It's not for the stage – it's for gang life.

With their army and influence rising it was time for their first big venture together. So, in the early eighties, Mackintosh and Lloyd Webber collaborated on the show *Cats*. Originally the show was just a whim of an idea because Lloyd Webber wanted to see Brian Blessed in a lycra catsuit. But as rehearsals developed they realised they were onto something which was going to be very special indeed.

Although rehearsals were rather erratic, and several members of the cast were threatened by competing gangs, things moved steadily forward. Mackintosh had employed one of the biggest 'heavies' in London to direct the show – knowing full well that if any other producer or gang stepped into the rehearsal room then this criminal boss would take them down. This director was on the run from the FBI and CIA, but had cleverly managed to disguise himself in two-tone denim and outrageous beard growth. Nowadays he goes by the name of Trevor 'Shooter' Nunn. Back then he was well known for killing actors who didn't understand his method, and castrating men so they could play girls in his Shakespeare productions.

The marvellous thing about Trevor was the respect he commanded – which complemented Mackintosh and Lloyd Webber perfectly. With Trevor in charge of *Cats* and drama schools producing the triple-threat army there would be no stopping them.

Nunn had been very shrewd in his casting of *Cats* – getting some of the toughest and most violent actors around. He had enlisted Bonnie 'Three Kills' Langford, Brian 'Squasher' Blessed and Elaine 'Pillaging' Paige. Not to mention the scariest of them all – Wayne 'The Silencer' Sleep. Add to that the most aggressive ensemble of dancers ever and *Cats* was a show not to be messed with.

Of course, everyone knows the story of Judi Dench famously having to leave *Cats* due to a 'torn Achilles tendon'. But that's just what was told to the press. In reality, Judi got on the wrong side of Trevor when she refused to partake in the company 'cat workshop' – which involved eating cat-food and using a litter tray for a week. Judi wasn't keen on the idea, and Trevor responded in the only fashion he knew – violence. Bless Judi. Although she was lucky. If Trevor had been *really* angry she wouldn't be with us today.

As a personal favour to Tim Rice, Trevor agreed to give the gig to Tim's favourite Soho girl – Elaine Paige. This was actually an excellent bit of casting as Elaine was the best pussy in the business, and her performance is talked about even today.

After what seemed like years of rehearsals, *Cats* opened to huge success. It was the first musical of its kind and, along with Mackintosh and Lloyd Webber's other shows, made them millions. Now they had success, money, whole theatre districts, and an acting army. They were ready to take over London completely. Until an unexpected Willy came on the scene.

Willy Russell was a man who had a different drive to Mackintosh and Lloyd Webber. He didn't particularly want his musical, that was being hugely successful on tour, to transfer to the West End. He felt that the West End of London wasn't his turf. But on hearing about the gang warfare, and Mackintosh and Lloyd Webber's bid to control London, he knew he had to do something. Being from Liverpool, Willy had already fought and won his fare share of battles – and was prepared to take on the might of these two criminal barbarians.

Blood Brothers was a show that Willy had written in 1982 – and was being very well received in the provinces. Lloyd Webber and Mackintosh had heard about Willy's reputation – and were justifiably afraid. Willy came with the same reputation as Trevor. They both had impressive facial hair. They both had style. They both had talent. But only one of them was from Liverpool. And that terrified Mackintosh.

The problem was that Mackintosh desired control of every single theatre in London. If a new person competed, and won one of the venues, then his reputation would be tarnished for ever.

If anyone was going to do it – it was Willy.

However, Willy knew that he couldn't take on the might and force of the Really Useful Mackintosh on his own, so he enlisted the help of another upcoming producer – Bill Kenwright. Kenwright had taken an interest in Willy for some time. He had actually been trying to convince Willy to bring *Blood Brothers* into London for years – but Willy had never felt the time was right. But the time was right now for their partnership – a partnership to try and save London's theatreland. Willy and Billy were ready.

One dark evening in the spring of 1983, Willy and Billy entered Dean Street with Barbara Dickson at their side. Willy was clutching the vocal score of *Blood Brothers*. Mackintosh and Lloyd Webber were at the other end of Dean Street with Elaine Paige, each of them holding the *Evita* vocal score. It was the start of the biggest theatrical war in history.

Word of this legendary battle spread far and wide, and every actor watched from afar. Willy was first to strike as he directed Barbara Dickson in a touching version of 'Marilyn Monroe' – so moving that Tim Rice fell to his knees in tears. Then Mackintosh responded with a tactical Elaine Paige move – a perky rendition of 'Rainbow High'. This took Willy by complete surprise and he was knocked aside by Paige's violent vibrato.

Barbara Dickson then relished the chance and delivered a deafening version of 'Tell Me It's Not True'. Soho got on its feet and applauded. Lloyd Webber was horrified. He realised 'Don't Cry for Me, Argentina' was no match for this, but forced Elaine to perform. She stood in her *Evita* pose, sucked on a lozenge, and sang for her life. It was the performance of her career, and the moment Lloyd Webber knew she was destined to play Norma Desmond.

Now it was Mackintosh and Billy's turn. The ultimate showdown. There was nothing else for it. A musical-theatre sing-off.

Billy rose to his feet and gallantly burst into a haunting rendition of 'Shoes Upon the Table'. At the same time, Cameron tore open his jacket, revealed his feline chest hair, and began singing 'Memory'. London went quiet. All were listening. Agents dropped their clients, casting directors dropped their boyfriends, and directors dropped their scripts. This was the theatrical sing-off of all time.

Billy desperately ball-changed as he sang, and Cameron got on all fours and meowed like a mad man. Barbara Dickson and Elaine Paige were engaged in one-on-one combat. It was a bloody, filthy, aural mess. 'Memory' and 'Shoes Upon the Table' should never be sung simultaneously. It was a musical travesty, a challenge to Doctor Theatre, a beckoning to the gods of drama. The singing intensified, Billy's vocal chords snapped, and Cameron's meowing intensified into a howl.

Then the miracle happened.

A bright light hovered above Soho and music screeched from the heavens. The doors of The Groucho Club burst open and a distant figure lurched forward. It was the man everyone feared. The man with the ultimate composing power. It was Stephen Sondheim.

Mackintosh and Billy froze. They were in the presence of the biggest Mafia leader of all time. Sondheim had all the gangs in the USA working for him – these two UK boys were no match.

'Mackintosh. Lloyd Webber. Willy. Billy. *Stop!* This is not what musical theatre is about. Theatre is an art. A craft. A reflection of humanity – and through your brutality you are trying to kill it. We are the creators of this live art. And we must work together. You will all be at peace. Otherwise I will never let you produce any of my work. Including *West Side Story*. Heed my advice. Or I will return with my army of Broadway boys.'

With that, Sondheim did a tremendous jazz-hand salute and ball-changed into The Ivy. And Soho was once again left in peace.

Mackintosh, Lloyd Webber, Willy and Billy's eyes met. They walked towards each other and held out their hands. Willy produced a knife from his pocket. Each man took turns cutting their palms with the blade. They then all did a bloody handshake and took an oath. They were now blood brothers.

In the weeks that followed, peace was once again restored to London. And, as a mark of forgiveness, *Blood Brothers* opened in the West End on the 11th April 1983 at the Lyric Theatre.

To this day Mackintosh, Lloyd Webber and Billy run London with their army of triple-threat actors. Their legacy has survived, and, thanks to them, London continues to produce the best theatre in the world.

And Willy? Well, *Blood Brothers* ran for twenty-four years in the West End – not bad considering he wasn't keen to bring it to London. Since then he's been writing, directing, and slowly morphing into a chubby Trevor Nunn. Bless, dear.

ACT THREE: PERFORMING

OR
TITS, ASS, TEETH, JAZZ HANDS, BALL-CHANGES, COSTUMES, BEGINNERS, STANDBY AND GO!

Actors – after a three-show day, when you have no voice, your body is weak, and you feel like death – remember you are living the dream, dear.

Performing

So you've auditioned, got the job and rehearsed, you've spent hours on the loo trying to learn your lines, you've got to know your fellow cast mates and spurned the advances of the sex pest (unless you are the sex pest), you've done a full runthrough, a technical rehearsal, a dress rehearsal, and have had far too many notes from your director – and now the time is here! It's performance time. This is the time when *you* are in control. As soon as you walk onto that stage it is all down to you. No one can tell you what to do, how to do it, and when to do it, apart from yourself. And that is a wonderful feeling. You deserve to be on that stage. It is also a very anxious and trusting time when you hope that the rest of the cast are going to do what was rehearsed. Because if they do not then you could be in trouble. That is the joy of performing – you never know what is going to happen. And if the worst does occur, and a fellow actor starts wetting themself downstage-centre, there is nothing you can do but watch. And laugh. And hope that none of it trickles onto the front row. Because that is live theatre. *Anything* can happen. And that is why we love it, dear!

Some actors say they love rehearsing, some actors say they love performing, and some actors say they love drinking. But personally, my favourite part is the performances. I love watching actors as they grace the stage for the first time and respond to an audience. I adore watching their performances grow and alter night after night after night. And I get incredibly emotional when I hear the rapturous applause of an audience as they enthusiastically respond to a show I have helped develop for weeks, months and years. It really is thrilling. The only time I don't like the performance is when the show is rubbish, and the audience hate it. When that happens you can find me in the bar, opening another bottle of Dom, and getting savagely sloshed, dear.

Let's have a look at the excitement and tribulations of performing. Starting with your first night. And what's the most important thing on the first night? The first-night present, of course.

The First-night Present

Many people in the industry get their priorities all wrong. As soon as they get offered a job they spend the next few months preparing for the role, doing research and learning their lines. Whilst this effort is not completely wasted, it is certainly a shame that they don't spend more time concentrating on the real priority. Namely, the first-night present.

The first-night present is a tradition that dates back many, many years – to one of the most memorable and theatrical nights ever. That first Nativity performance when Jesus was born in a stable was a monumental piece of theatre. It was lit so beautifully by the Star of Bethlehem, and had a wonderful set designed by shepherds. And when the Three Wise Men presented Jesus with gold, frankincense and myrrh, it marked the beginning of the 'first-night present' tradition.

A first-night present can change everything. People are judged on many things – the most important being the size, value and originality of the present. Of course, now that times are hard and some actors are forced to take work that pays as little as £0 a week (or minus figures if it's a 'profit share'), it may become necessary to remortgage your house to participate in this touching and important discipline. And I think, in time, you will realise it is money well spent.

When choosing a present it is essential you consider what is expected. There is no point buying someone a bra and panties as this could be deemed inappropriate. However, if the bra and panties are branded with the show's logo then you could become the most popular person in your company.

There was a time when all that was expected was a card. And in some companies this is still okay. But there will always be an air of disappointment and bitterness if everyone else goes to the trouble and expense of buying a gift and you do not. It can take years of buying drinks in the pub to make up for this error of judgement.

You don't have to buy everyone a different present – and often this is a wise decision, as favouritism will then be judged on the expense of the gift. In fact, it can be very sweet and thoughtful if you get everyone the same thing. However, if you do this, you *must* make the cards personal.

No one likes a card that reads 'It's been great working with you.' This smacks of insincerity and lacks any sense of personality – indeed, you could be writing the card to someone you've only just met. It is essential you remember something funny that happened in rehearsals, or if that fails, just make something up.

If you are extra keen on the present and card tradition you could take the 'stalking' route and find as much information about every cast member as possible by asking their friends and ex-partners, or by reading their diaries. Of course, this will take up a lot of time – and may result in you getting a restraining order, but you will be very well-respected for your 'first-night initiative'.

Some of the most bizarre first-night presents I have received over the years include:

- A full-body massage by six members of the male ensemble.

- A pet snake called Cameron.

- Fifteen signed copies of Craig Revel Horwood's autobiography.

- A year's membership to the *Fiddler on the Roof* Appreciation Society.

- A signed sculpture of John Barrowman's willy.

- The greatest hits of Marti Pellow.

- A *Miss Saigon* blow-up doll (which has been surprisingly useful).

Never make the mistake of only buying for the cast. This is highly inappropriate and will get you a bad reputation with everybody else involved in the show. There are so many people to buy for – backstage crew, wardrobe, dressers, stage-door keepers, lighting designers, resident directors, musical directors, cleaners, wig-makers, writers, second cousins of the director, the director's children, the musical director's wife and, most importantly, the producer. Be certain that no one is left out. Obviously it is most important to buy for the director, casting director and producer – as they are the ones who will be hiring you again. This is essential to remember – always be thinking of your next job, dear.

When playing drunks, try to remain sober – otherwise you'll forget how to play drunk properly, dear.

The Company Warm-up

Many actors get confused, irritated and ashamed at the prospect of a company warm-up before a show. They feel that this simple and helpful pastime undermines them as performers – as why should they be forced to warm up? Surely, they argue, the responsibility of warming up relies on the actors themselves – and if they feel warm enough then they should be excluded from this tradition. I'm afraid I disagree. Whilst I see the point that actors are quite capable of warming up by themselves, the sad truth is they hardly do. If I were to excuse all of my casts from warming up there would be a nation of cold, lifeless actors jumping around on stage every night. And that is only excusable when doing Ibsen, dear.

An actor may argue that they have already been to the gym, had a singing lesson, spent two hours in their local toilets, and been rubbed down by their various partners. Whilst I appreciate that this makes them warm, it does not make them feel involved and included with the rest of the company – which is precisely the point of the company warm-up.

A company warm-up is not mandatory in every show and, indeed, in some companies it is not even considered. However, it is commonplace in musicals and bigger physical shows that a warm-up takes place. It is a necessary part of an actor's schedule – as not only does it warm and prepare you for the show, but allows the whole company to come together as one.

This is particularly important for big shows, when a warm-up is often the only time the entire company are together. In these kinds of shows you are in a big theatre, littered in dressing rooms at the extremities of the building, and may never be on stage with everyone else in the company. Whilst this can be comforting (particularly if you don't like your fellow cast members), it can also be quite disconcerting – particularly when performing in an ensemble show.

'Ensemble' is a word that is flung around theatres almost as much as John Barrowman. It is quoted by everyone – and all good directors will mention the word at least five times an hour. It instils an actor with a sense of belonging and purpose – as though they are performing with a close-knit band of brothers and family members. But, of course, they are not. They are generally performing with recently graduated *Fame* fanatics who only care about progressing up the career ladder. But by the suggestive use of the word 'ensemble', an actor is made to feel at home.

In essence, an ensemble theatre piece means every member of the company is important and has a vital role to play in the show – whether they are saying one word or 1,500 lines. Of course, this is utter nonsense. The most important person in a show is the lead. That is quite obvious. If we have a marvellous lead, the show stands much more chance of being a huge success. If we have a member of the ensemble who says two words, to be honest, it doesn't really matter if they're bad. It won't have that much effect on the whole show. Obviously it helps if they can speak without dribbling and vomiting, but the audience will quickly forget about it anyway, dear.

Actors – please avoid warming up in the bedroom. Particularly when I'm asleep, dear.

The Dance Captain

Dance captains are a rare breed of performer who are employed to take physical warm-ups and make sure the choreography stays up to standard. They can be spotted a mile off by the fact that they will be wearing as little as possible, have a six pack, and can contort themselves into a ball the size of Craig Revel Horwood's nose. Dance captains will have studied all disciplines of dance, and will excel in anything that involves extreme discomfort – and take huge delight in forcing this pain onto other members of the company. They will also be highly experienced in the art of 'domination', and supplement their income by whipping nappy-wearing lawyers and doctors at the weekend.

Dance captains will never admit this, but they are always in cahoots with the company manager, who in turn is in cahoots with me. It is really rather marvellous hearing stories about the company warm-up and how certain actors are more resourceful and enthusiastic than others. Indeed, recently I have started to make my deputy stage managers take a register at the beginning of warm-ups – for no other reason than to make the actors feel like they are back at school. This is marvellous for discipline, and is useful in reminding actors that they must be on their best behaviour at all times, and abide by the School of Theatre Rules.

The School of Theatre Rules

1 No running in the wings.

2 Respect the 'creatives'.

3 No physical violence.

4 Wear your costume on stage at all times.

5 Look after your dressing room, making sure it is tidy for routine inspections.

6 There must be complete silence during the notes session.

7 Single file when walking to the stage.

8 Keep to the right.

9 Be in place and have your character ready when the show demands it.

10 No actor may remain in the theatre overnight without prior permission.

11 The sucking of sweets is prohibited on stage. That's what your dressing room is for.

12 No heavy petting.

13 No diving.

14 The ensemble and understudies must be silent when the principals demand it.

15 No actor may enter another dressing room apart from their own without written permission.

16   All show-pants must be returned to wardrobe stain-free.

17   Always arrive early for the company warm-up with a bottle of water for hydration.

18   In case of emergency, actors must be labelled with their agent's details.

19   Actors who are late must report to the company manager, where necessary discipline will be administered.

20   Actors' detention will commence after the performance (see pages 138–39).

21   A sick note, photographic evidence of your illness and a urine sample is required for shows missed.

22   During every term there will be a show 'Open Day' – where cast members' parents are invited to speak to the director, casting director, producer and musical director about their behaviour and development.

23   No smoking. Except at stage door. Or out of your dressing-room window. Or on stage (in Noël Coward plays).

24   No drinking alcohol before a matinee or evening show – unless you really need it.

25   'I'm only on Equity minimum' is not a valid excuse for stealing goods of any kind.

26   'Character choices' must not leave the theatre without written permission.

27   You must put your hand in the air and warn everyone if you are going to be creative.

Hopefully the entire company will be following Rule 17 and be present at the warm-up wearing suitable attire (and carrying a water bottle). I am always shocked at what people choose to wear in company warm-ups – it frequently becomes a competition to see who wears the most revealing clothing. Invariably the dance captain wins this contest by wearing nothing apart from pants and nipple tassels, followed by envious ensemble members who favour tight crop-tops. My casting director often visits the warm-up under the pretence that he needs to have a chat with everyone. He doesn't. He just likes staring and dribbling.

The physical warm-up will consist of ten to twenty minutes of physical movement. This will involve moves as varied as lunges, ball-changes, and desperate stretching to the ceiling. There will inevitably be a section where the entire company try and do the splits – which can be rather messy, particularly after a big night out.

Some dance captains will vary their warm-up day by day, and others will do exactly the same thing for years. It doesn't really matter what they do, as long as they make everyone jump up and down to alert their naughty bits that they are about to do a show.

Some dance captains will even occasionally play the latest Natalie Cassidy Fitness DVD during the warm-up – not so everyone can follow her moves, but so everyone can have a good laugh.

I always find it interesting to be informed about who stands in the back row in the physical warm-up. These people are the perverted members of the company who do pathetic little stretches whilst staring at everyone's bottoms. This is rather uncomfortable, particularly when it is the older cast members. I remember a specific incident when one Fagin used to leave warm-ups with an obvious erection. It was terribly embarrassing, particularly as it didn't go down for the duration of the show – and gave a whole new meaning to 'You've Got to Pick a Pocket or Two'.

Next will follow the vocal warm-up, usually taken by the musical director. However, if the musical director is not available, the assistant musical director will do it. And if he isn't available an overenthusiastic actor will offer their services. This is always embarrassing and results in feelings of anger and resentment in the rest of the company.

The vocal warm-up will consist of humming, a few scales, a little sing-song and some tongue-twisters. You should expect to use the words 'me may mah more moo' frequently, and it is a mortal sin if you don't know the many variations of 'Bella Signora'. One of the main aims of the vocal warm-up is to avoid looking like a blow-up doll. Obviously you have to open your mouth – but always be aware of how open it actually is. As a rule, aim for two fingers fitting into your mouth – as this is the perfect size for warming up, singing and acting in general. Never, ever try and put your whole hand in, as no one wants to see an actor fisting themselves.

Examples of Tongue-twisters

- Red lorry, yellow lorry, red lorry, yellow lorry.

- Unique New York, New York unique, unique New York, New York unique.

- A proper cup of coffee from a proper copper coffee pot, a proper cup of coffee from a proper copper coffee pot.

- Equity minimum, Equity million, Equity minimum, Equity million.

- Actors actually act excellently, actors actually act excellently.

- Stella Adler, Stella Kowalski, Stella Artois, Stella Adler, Stella Kowalski, Stella Artois.

- Louie Spence on a fence is tense like a tent, Louie Spence on a fence is tense like a tent.

- Equity deputy, Equity jeopardy, Equity deputy, Equity jeopardy.

- John Michael Ball Barrowman, Michael John Barrowman Ball, John Michael Ball Barrowman, Michael John Barrowman Ball.

Even if you can't actually do the tongue-twisters, you should always pretend that you can. That's what everyone else will be doing.

If you ever feel uncomfortable during the vocal warm-up and worry that your voice isn't good enough, you must always remember that you will never be the worst-sounding person in the room. That will be the musical director. Bless them. That's why they are a musical director and not a performer. For the occasional treat, and to make yourself feel better, just ask the musical director to demonstrate one of their exercises. When you hear their tight, squeaky singing voice you will be instantly reminded of how talented you really are.

It is always advisable to do your warm-up before the show, and not in the bar afterwards, dear.

Before the Show

At the end of the warm-up everyone looks around the room and makes sure the dance captain has still got their pants on – and then the company manager makes some announcements. Announcements tend to be rather boring affairs like who is off, which understudy is on, and which actors need to be better. Sometimes there are birthday announcements – which are embarrassing affairs where the entire company spontaneously burst into a rousing rendition of 'Happy Birthday'. Of course, this includes lots of complicated harmony and at least three key changes, as everyone uses it to show off their skill, and to remind the musical director of how gifted they are.

If it's a long-running show, especially a musical, a resident director will then give some notes. They will tell you, in their opinion, how the show is looking from 'out front', what needs work, and when someone important is going to be watching. It is vital you listen to this – as your resident director will inform you when the 'proper' director is in. When this happens it is essential you do the show exactly the way it was originally directed. This can be very challenging, and in some cases impossible, as the show will have changed so much that it is now unrecognisable. This is when your company manager will save the day and play a recording of what the show used to look like.

A good resident director will then give a pep talk about making the show as good as possible. An even better resident director will say nothing at all and just let you get on with it.

Any company notes session will be taken by the director, assistant director, resident director, associate director, assistant to the associate director, resident's assistant director, supervisor to the director, or any other person we can find. When you get a note from the original director it is advisable to take the note and do what he or she says. If any of the other directors give you a note, just nod your head – and carry on doing what you were doing anyway. It makes them feel important, you appear grateful, and is the best solution for everyone involved.

After all of the above it will nearly be the half-hour call – so if you need a fag or some food you should make a last-minute dash to the local shop. Or simply order a pizza or curry to be delivered in the interval.

Of course, sometimes doing a physical and vocal warm-up is just far too draining and time-consuming – and on days like this I recommend doing a company 'Gangnam Style'.

....

Two of my cast were caught having naughty fun in a dressing room. I've given them a written warning to lock the door next time, dear.

....

Quick Changes

Quick changes are often a bone of contention and many actors don't know the correct way of dealing with them. For one thing, you should always be sure to wear underwear (unless you are trying the 'no-pants technique', see page 135) – as it can be rather embarrassing having your naughty bits flapping about backstage. You may have a dresser to make your task more pleasant, in which case they will be used to seeing your naughty bits – and will have seen so many that they will have become immune to them. Wardrobe mis-tresses will always scold you for not wearing show-pants, though, as they play the important role of preventing skid-marks going onto expensive and unwashable costumes.

Obviously at the beginning of the run your quick changes will take a lot longer than when you have mastered them. Indeed, quick changes are usually the things that slow tech-nical rehearsals down more than anything else. Actors never want to feel like they may be forced to make a dramatic entrance wearing nothing but a jockstrap or thong. Unless they are John Barrowman.

The thing to remember is to remain calm. It is much easier doing a quick change when you take your time than when you rush around and get your legs stuck in your arm-holes. I remember a funny incident in a production of *Macbeth* in the eighties where, after an unsuccessful quick change, the only thing covering Macbeth's naughty bits was the dagger from his 'Is this a dagger I see before me?' speech. The problem was that the dagger was being mimed, meaning that the audience had a perfect view of Macbeth's 'naughty instrument'. Mind you, this little accident didn't do the box office any harm – word spread that it was the most 'revealing' *Macbeth* in history and the production completely sold out, confirming what we all knew anyway: nudity sells. Even in Shakespeare.

Tipping dressers, just like bullying the understudies, is an old theatrical tradition. There is no hard-and-fast rule about it – and many performers don't believe in the tradition now, stating that dressers 'get just as much money as us actors'. But you should always remember that one day you will also be a dresser, and will be hugely appreciative of the extra coppers given to you. Also, tipping a dresser is tax deductible – it's a professional expense!

Some actors don't listen properly. I told one yesterday to wait for a pause, not applause.

Bowing

Every actor needs a good bow. It is essential in completing a performance, and is the perfect opportunity to show the audience your appreciation. Even if you give a terrible performance in a bloody awful show, a marvellous bow can redeem everything.

I have always been appalled that drama schools don't dedicate a term to the 'art of bowing' – and some don't even offer a workshop in this specialised field. It is a great tragedy, and is the main reason why the general standard of bowing has deteriorated over the years. I remember the good old days when bows would involve jazz hands, ball-changes and the exchange of bodily fluids – and became the highlight of a show. I must admit sometimes the bows are still my favourite part, but that's only because I'm thrilled that the show's over.

A bow completes your performance, and shows the audience what kind of actor you are – and without a good one, an actor looks like a flailing amateur.

There have been many heated debates over the years about the correct approach to bowing, and whether you should still be 'in character'. Many people believe that it is the one time when you can truly be yourself, allowing the audience to see you as *you*. Other, more Method actors tend to think you should always be in character. Personally, I don't mind – as long as actors stay in their costume. It is not appropriate to take a bow in your own clothes – even if you have to dash off to catch your train.

Some more 'arty' directors get rid of the bow completely – as they think it leaves a far stronger impact on the audience. For some reason they think that bringing the actors back on stage shatters the show's illusion, and ruins everything that has gone before. To these directors I say 'Grow up.' By not allowing the actors to bow you are denying them of their right to bow, and the audience of their right to applaud.

There are different time limits when bowing – and the greater your role in the show, the longer you are allowed. Obviously you will know your status within the company by when your bow is. If you bow first in the curtain call then you are the least important actor – but if you are fortunate enough to take the final bow you are the most important actor and are entitled to take as long as you wish, ranging from two minutes to two hours. I have witnessed many bows, particularly at the National, that have lasted as long as the performance itself. Some people call this indulgent. I call it talent.

You see, a bow is like another show in itself. And if an artist can keep an audience entertained by doing a two-hour bow then they should be applauded. Personally, I never understand why actors don't take bows at the end of films. It would be thrilling to see Sigourney Weaver and her monsters taking a lovely long curtain call at the end of *Alien*, dear.

Bowing, in simple terms, requires you to bend. In showbusiness, and in theatre particularly, there are lots of highly experienced benders. I know many benders who have been practising since early adolescence, and still feel their bend is not perfect. A good bender will have studied and researched the history of bowing, and will have spent many long evenings in the company of other benders. Between them these benders share hints, tips, and bending techniques to try and find the perfect bend. Sometimes it is only through the gentle force of another bender that the inexperienced bender can feel comfortable with the thrilling, yet sometimes painful bending sensation.

Of course, bowing/bending in some countries is used as a form of greeting, and a gesture of respect. And the different forms of bowing can be used to express different emotions – from sincerity, gratitude, humility and sexual attraction (particularly if you are bowing directly to the groin region). So it has a very powerful and significant history. Which is why the simple act of bowing should not be treated simply at all.

Generally, as an actor, your bow should show respect and appreciation to the audience. You are showing them you are grateful that they came, supported and, most importantly, came back for the second half. I think it particularly pertinent in today's society, when there are so many shows to choose from, a bow is a way of saying 'Thank you for coming to see the one I'm in.' You should always remember that the audience is actually your employer. Without them there would be no show, so your bow is thanking them for your wages. If you are only getting Equity minimum then you may not want to show much appreciation.

How you bow depends entirely on what you want to convey, and when you are bowing. If your bow is early in the curtain call you should try not to be self-indulgent, as a bow that is too long can smack of desperation and overenthusiasm. As a general rule, an early bow should be short, sharp and succinct – just like Andrew Lloyd Webber's forehead. You should aim for a strong, confident walk to centre-stage, look straight ahead, then lower your torso and head in one swift, smooth motion. Aim to get your head no lower then your belly button – as any lower can result in it looking like you're trying to give yourself a blow job. Then come straight back up, and do a little nod of the head to finish it off. If you felt they were a particularly good audience you can, of course, flick your right hand in the air behind you as you bow. This can look smart, elegant or just plain foolish – depending on the angle of your arm. So I suggest a little bit of practice in front of a mirror beforehand.

If you are bowing at the same time as a lot of other actors then you have two options. One is that everyone does the same bow – and looks wonderfully regimented. The other is that you all do your own personal bows, in an attempt to pull focus. Personally, I think it a lot more fun if you adopt the 'pulling focus' technique. This is your time, the time when the audience are applauding your talent – so you should do all you can to try and make them look at you. There are many ways to try and outdo each other, but you shouldn't try and make it too obvious as this can cause tension backstage. If you are all running down in a line it can be rather fun to do a little jump before going into your bow – this will immediately bring the audience's focus onto you. If you are feeling particularly cheesy a little pat on your heart and humble nodding of the head can go down a treat. Then, as everyone else begins to bow, do the opposite and look to the upper circle with arms outstretched before graciously lowering your head to your hips. As you bend, try taking both hands up behind you in a salute to the upper circle. They will appreciate this and also the actors either side of you will have no idea what you are doing. Then come up smoothly and give the audience a little wink. If you do all of this you will definitely pull focus and show your true bending talent. However, you may not have time to do this – in which case you should just do a quick nod to the audience, blow them a kiss, and then bow. Either way you will look marvellously theatrical.

Sometimes you will be faced with the task of bowing with someone you don't like, or in severe cases, someone you despise – and usually this person will be playing your lover. If this is the case you should remember to use the well known 'bow-hand gestures'. Traditionally the man will bow first and then gesture for his lady to bow. If you do not get on with your co-star you can signal it on your other hand. Your thumb pointing downwards means they are difficult, your middle finger pointing down means they are a nightmare, and your first two fingers pointing down in a v-shape means they are the devil. This is a useful tool – particularly for those audience members in the industry – as it makes us understand how difficult the whole process has been for you.

Now we come to the star's bow. The star will always have the final bow in the curtain call. If they are particularly nice the rest of the company will applaud when the star walks down. Obviously this is not compulsory and is only done when the company feels the star deserves it. In honesty, the worst thing to see is half of the company applauding and the other half refusing – making the whole thing look rather awkward.

Once the star has hit their spot they will take a few minutes to look around the auditorium. A very well-known dramatist once said that when bowing you should try and look at everyone in the audience. Clearly this was said as a generalisation, but some stars take it upon themselves to follow it through to the bitter end. In which case you are in for a very long night indeed.

Sometimes the star will blow kisses to the audience – particularly if they are getting a standing ovation. Then they may gesture to a friend in the audience, miming drinking a pint. Often the star will then mime 'thank you' back to the audience in a patronising and insincere way.

A very important rule when bowing is that you can never bow for longer than the amount of dialogue you say in the show. So if you are a small part and say one line you are confined to a very short and sharp bow. However, when you are playing the lead this means you can take for ever. Unless, of course, you are doing a mime piece, in which case this rule is null and void.

So the star will invariably take their time. After the obligatory gestures to the audience, and condescending nods to the rest of the cast, they will start lowering their head. A true star will never take their eyes from the audience – they will always be staring out front during their bow. In fact, some stars take this eye-contact rule so seriously that they decide not to lower their heads at all, and just do a very deep knee-bend instead. This can look marvellous and give the appearance of a beautiful plié, or it can give the ungainly appearance of someone taking a centre-stage shit. This is something that you have to judge for yourself, depending on what kind of costume you are wearing. Of course, there is the risk that you could get stuck in this kind of a bow and need assistance by another member of the company. I witnessed this incident when a very well-known dame got stuck in her 'knee-bending' bow and would not ask for assistance from anyone. In the end she just fell onto her side and rolled herself offstage. In truth, there was something strangely poetic about the whole ritual.

Many stars will, of course, take a lot longer than this – or use different bowing techniques. Sometimes the star will even decide to take three bows, one aimed at each side of the auditorium – the middle, stage-right, and stage-left. This can be very effective when playing bigger theatres, but can be very embarrassing when playing a small fringe venue with an audience of four.

It is important to remember that the deeper your bow, the more appreciation you are showing the audience. So if they were good, or you had someone special watching then it is advisable to do a deep bow. A deep bow is one where your forehead goes anywhere between your groin region and knees. An extremely deep bow is when your head goes anywhere below your knees, showing very deep gratitude. Over the years I have seen some extraordinarily deep bows where the forehead is literally banging on the actor's big toe. Whilst this does look marvellous, it is only advisable for performers in Cirque du Soleil.

A new kind of bow which has become very trendy of late (particularly in avant-garde companies) is the backward bow. Upon first glance this bow can seem rather rude, but on completion is an absolute delight. Basically the actor runs to the front of the stage, turns around, tenses their buttocks – and does an extremely deep bow facing upstage. All the audience can see is the back of the actor, giving them a marvellous view of their bottom – which is usually a terrific sight in its own right. Indeed, I have been to many shows where this has been the highlight. Then, as the actor takes his deep bend he very slowly parts his legs and his face is revealed – upside down – hanging between his legs! This is a joy to see – and backward-bow virgins tend to find the whole experience life-changing. Of course, when you are hanging there you can smile, thank the audience, and even attempt to lick your bottom (but not when doing a schools tour). Then the actor slowly rises up to his standing position, turns round, and is greeted with even more applause by the audience. I hope to see more backward bows in the future, dear.

A word of warning: Overenthusiasm can be dangerous – particularly when bowing. Bowing is one of the most dangerous sports there is – and insurance companies will not cover you for bowing-related injuries. A common accident is whiplash, which occurs when an actor is far too energetic and, upon reaching his upright position, whips his head back. So be warned: never whip your head back too dramatically.

Another regular accident is the knee-knock, which occurs when lowering your head into a bow. Again, overenthusiasm causes the actor to bow far too quickly resulting in them headbutting their knees. Which in itself can be awful – but is even more awful when both knees protrude into the eye sockets. Not nice at all. And a bugger for the make-up artist who has to cover your two black eyes for the next month.

So always be careful – and remember the signs of a bad bow by following the 'FAST' rule:

Fast – Never be too fast in the lead-up to a bow.

Anus – It is vital to have a tight anus at all times. This is essential in controlling your bow, and helps prevent unnecessary leakages.

Smile – It is recommended to smile at least once during a bow. If you spot someone not smiling, please smile for them.

Technique – If you spot an actor with a terrible bowing technique you must do the honourable thing and drag them offstage. A bad bow can ruin an entire show, and stain every other actor's reputation. It is the bow captain's responsibility to check the whole company's bows at least twice a week.

Recently I was told by a young actor how to use your bow cleverly to get you a date. During the show you will undoubtedly have spent most of the time looking into the audience trying to spot the gorgeous people. In the interval all the cast will convene in the green room and chat about which girl is gorgeous, and which boy is beautiful – and where these people are sitting in the audience. During the second half the cast will try and spot the 'hotties' that the other cast members have recommended. This game can be much fun, and very rewarding – but do be careful not to make it too obvious. There was an actor in Blackpool that had such a good view of one lady's cleavage that he involuntarily dribbled right into the middle of it. It wouldn't have been so bad, but she was the director's wife, dear.

The 'get a date' bow requires you to prepare a little piece of card with your name, phone number and dressing-room number on. As you walk downstage, stare at the person you fancy – and as you stand up from your bow when your arms naturally swing forward let your hand flick and spin the card to your potential date. Hopefully your aim will be spot-on and you will be in for a marvellous evening. However, if your aim is off by 10cm you could find yourself taking out a night-shift worker from the local chicken factory.

The sun has got his hat on, hip hip hip hooray. But we can't get a suntan as we've got a matinee.

Press Night

'For me, the press night is like climaxing after weeks of gentle intercourse. Auditions are when I partake in some light foreplay with potential lovers. Rehearsals are when I make gentle love to everyone in the company as I get to know them all. And the press night is when I climax. Then I light a fag, relax and fall asleep.' An anonymous director

Press nights are remarkable affairs. They are what the actors and production team have been working towards for the whole of the rehearsal period, and with them comes immense pressure – they are the one night when it is essential not to *fuck it up.*

The smooth running of a press night is usually handled by a PR company, who will have been employed months in advance to help with the whole marketing aspect of the show. They will be in charge of media, interviews, press, invitations, posters, images, social media, websites and John Barrowman's teeth.

It is absolutely vital that actors learn their lines by press night. There is nothing worse than hearing an actor shout 'Line' in front of all the critics and invited peers. It is such a fundamental mistake, and one which is often forgotten by some of our leading actors. It is not acceptable. Particularly when they've had the whole of the preview period to learn them.

Because of all the extra excitement on press nights, actors often overcompensate. I have seen actors down large amounts of Red Bull before heading on stage – which has caused them to tremble throughout their entire performance. This is how the actor playing Alfie, the old waiter in *One Man, Two Guvnors*, perfected his shaking. It was nothing to do with physical practice, it was just Red Bull shakes, dear.

It is extremely important that you look good during the curtain call on press night. Recently there has been a trend for photographers to take photos during it, and the following day you don't want your sweaty, rouge-smudged face appearing all over the internet. It is advisable to double-, triple- and quadruple-check before gliding onto the stage for your applause. Also, at the party there will be lots of press and photographers vying for your attention, desperate to get a marvellous shot – again making it essential you look immaculate. But as well as looking good it is wise to make sure you stand out. I suggest ladies wear a revealing dress or stylish onesie. And gents wear a tight suit that elegantly shows off their package.

The greatest moment about the press night is, of course, the party. These are usually lavish affairs that take place in wonderfully expensive locations where wine and beer is free-flowing and the nibbles are expensively inedible (unless you are doing a small-scale tour – where the party will be a pint of lager and bag of nuts in Wetherspoon's).

In honesty, I much prefer going to other people's press-night parties than my own. At my own parties I am forced to hang around the bar making sure that greedy actors and naughty front-of-house staff don't nick all the free booze. These affairs are always ridiculously hard on the wallet, particularly when Louie Spence swans around, sipping free champagne and gorging on nibbles and nipples all night.

I love nothing more than searching through my wardrobe before a press night. It takes hours of grooming and several costume changes before I look right, especially now that I 'theme' myself depending on what show I am going to see. Over the years my collection of different 'themed' pants has become quite extensive – ranging from my *Miss Saigon* thong to my *Phantom* Pampers. I sometimes even get a wardrobe mistress to make me some new ones if I am feeling particularly excited. Of course, no one gets to see my themed pants unless they ask very nicely after plying me with lots of Dom, dear.

I have spoken to many actors who find the whole process of mingling at parties rather disheartening. They lack the confidence to go and introduce themselves to the important people, and have a fear of appearing desperate. But, of course, they are not *expected* to do any of this – in fact, the important people will go to *them* if they think they've done a good job. If, however, you find yourself in an awkward position and no one is speaking to you, the best thing to do is pretend to be an agent. You will notice that everyone in the room suddenly starts mingling with you. And as a bonus you won't have to buy any drinks for the rest of the night. The only downside to this is when other actors from your show ask you to represent them. When this happens you must politely decline, and tell them that you don't think they're good enough.

Traffic-light Dating

You have to be careful what you wear at press-night parties for an important reason: traffic-light dating. Press-night parties are now more than just a theatrical event, they are specialised dating experiences, and are the ideal opportunity for single (or even taken) people to meet like-minded professionals.

In truth, this is the reason so many critics, casting directors and well-known actors go to press nights – in the hope that they might find potential intimate encounters. Of course, there are rules to these evenings, and you should be made fully aware of them before engaging in this form of social intercourse. There is nothing worse than turning up to a press night wearing a colour that is entirely inappropriate.

Traffic-light Dating Colour Code

Red informs interested parties to 'stop' – as you are taken. People in red will usually be in a relationship, or will have taken a vow of chastity after having far too many messy and intimate encounters whilst on tour. You should approach these kinds of people with extreme caution, as any sort of social dialogue that even hints at the bedroom will result in the heavy use of pepper spray.

Yellow is the 'ambiguous' colour – and informs interested parties that you are *possibly* available. It means you will be open to certain offers with certain people, although you reserve the right to terminate an agreement if the predator proposes something too ambitious. Yellow-clothed people tend to be rather non-specific about their sexuality and desires. As a general rule, all casting directors favour this colour.

Green signals 'Go!' – and informs everyone that you are a bit of a slapper who is up for anything. People who wear green are available, looking for a good time, and are not fussy. They are very open-minded, and will usually be married to someone who is not directly involved in the business, so they use press nights as the perfect way of broadening their intimate encounters. Green-clothed people are also often into swinging, and will bring a young, eager actor along to use as bait for potential suitors. Most agents favour this colour.

It is particularly important that cast members wear the correct colours on their press night – as they are the people that everyone is interested in. There is nothing worse than embarrassing a casting director who has spent an hour talking to you only for them to realise that you are not actually up for anything.

Usually your agent will have bribed, begged, and screamed down the phone at you to ensure you bring them as your press-night guest. It is an extremely important night – and you should obviously give your two complimentary tickets to the people that have supported, funded and helped carve your career out from a young age – but, of course, your agents won't care about this and will expect you to give the tickets to them. Cheeky buggers.

If you do take your agent it is your responsibility to keep an eye on them at all times and make sure they don't embarrass themselves by poaching and touching the other actors. Agents are notorious for hogging the bar area, and usually resort to extreme violence when the free alcohol runs out. *Your* agent is *your* responsibility – never forget this. If they get out of hand and start shouting at other agents it is *you* who will look embarrassed and inexperienced. However, if your agent is a member of the PMA (Personal Managers' Association) they will be easier to keep an eye on as they are tagged, and can never be more than half a mile outside of Soho.

During the press-night party you will inevitably get asked many tedious questions about the play and your involvement in it. Sadly these questions cannot be avoided, and you should do your best to answer them with as much positivity and enthusiasm as possible. Of course, this will often require a lot of lying, particularly in shows where you hate the rest of the cast. There are obvious techniques to help when answering questions like this – one of the most important is smiling, even if it's through gritted teeth. A smile will make everyone think that you have had a glorious rehearsal period full of laughter and support.

However, if you accidentally start slagging off a fellow member of your cast it is essential that you also laugh wildly – as this makes it look like you are joking. Of course, everyone will know that you are not, but at least it allows you to cover your back when you get interrogated about it the next day.

Obviously the most important person to ensure you thank and praise is the director – even if they are terrible – as they are the people who will employ you again. And, to be honest, you should never judge a director by how good they actually are at directing. I have known some bloody awful directors in my time, many of whom have gone on to run some of the best theatres in the country.

Never hand out business cards during press nights. This smacks of desperation. Everyone will know who you are and that you were in the show – and if they don't you should just break into song and dance and perform your audition pieces. Everyone loves an actor who is good at entertaining the crowd. Craig Revel Horwood does it all the time, usually climaxing in a naughty little strip. And I can tell you – his selection of themed show-pants is even bigger than mine, dear.

Actors – respect those that light, dress and mic you. Without them, you're a naked mute in the dark.

Backstage Etiquette

Over the years I have had the misfortune of reading many a show report stating how badly an actor has behaved. I understand that, like anyone, actors can get annoyed and frustrated – but hijacking props, and using the wig room as a toilet is not very considerate. If you have a problem in a company the best thing to do is seek your company manager and get them to deal with the situation. If you have a problem with your company manager, then unfortunately you are screwed. The company manager is someone who is trustworthy, efficient and good at their job. Either that or they're my friend.

Always treat your dressing room with the same amount of respect as your home. It should be a place where you can find sanctuary, peace, relaxation and fornication. And the way you treat it should reflect that. It is no good letting old food rot in the corner, and leaving unwashed pants on the floor – as that tends to attract mice, lice and Michael Barrymore.

Obviously some of you will be unfortunate enough to have to share a dressing room. Whilst this may be uncomfortable, it is sadly unavoidable. We can't have the celebrities spending more time than necessary with the ensemble – there's Equity rules about that. If you are in the ensemble, then chances are you'll be sharing a space of around four square feet with at least five other people. And that's only in the bigger theatres. I always think you should look upon it as a challenge. It's always good getting to know other actors – even if they clip their toenails in your seat and sing 'A Spoonful of Sugar' on loop.

You should always be assigned a little table space in front of a mirror. If you are very lucky you will have lights around the mirror. And if you are extra, extra lucky you will have a wash basin and fridge. The wash basin should *only* be used to wash in, and not to crouch over when the toilet is engaged. And the fridge should only be used to store food, and not to hide your children in. When you know where your place is, most actors like putting up cards and photos around the mirror. I would advise keeping the number of photos of yourself to a minimum, as it is not good to appear too self-obsessed.

If you are sharing a dressing room with someone you don't like, it can be tough. You should always try and get along with everyone. You are an actor – and that is your responsibility. Making enemies can result in constant regret, as that person could one day be running the National Theatre or your local Lidl. So I suggest doing your best to get to know the person. Take them out for drinks, get them drunk, find out if they've ever had a yeast infection, and bribe them. If that doesn't work, just tell them you're represented by Curtis Brown or United and they will show you nothing but respect.

When backstage you should always do your best to get on with the crew. These people are easily identifiable as the ones permanently dressed in funeral attire. They are mostly very nice people, and will be the ones who hand you your props and make sure the set is working correctly. It is a very courageous person who angers the crew, as it can result in serious implications to your health. Things could be dropped on you, wrong props could be given to you, and worst of all – you could be badly lit.

On many occasions you will find a dresser is assigned to you. A dresser plays an important role in the function of your day-to-day theatre life. They dress you, iron your clothes, talk to you, and on special occasions will play with you. Many dressers are resting actors – and should be treated with respect. Other dressers are not resting actors – and should be ignored. It is always advisable to get on with your dresser, otherwise you could find yourself on stage with no trousers, no bra, or simply naked. I will never forget the performance of *Les Misérables* where 'Bring Him Home' was performed entirely in the nude. It served him right for not getting his dresser a birthday present, dear.

If you are not in the theatre by the half-hour call then you are in trouble, unless you are the star – in which case we will make an exception to any rule you wish. The half-hour call is there so we can get the understudies ready if there is an emergency. To be honest, we never want an understudy to go on, but should the worst happen and we are forced to put one on, then it is essential they are prepared. An understudy must know all the lines of the person they are covering, and preferably in the right order. They must also know the moves, and be able to copy the original actor's performance. There is a misconception that an understudy can make the performance their own – they can, as long as they don't do anything differently. To be honest, we just want understudies to stand in the right place, say the right line, and get offstage so the audience don't notice.

I always advise actors to remember when they're wearing a radio microphone. A radio mic picks up everything you say and, although sound operators aren't meant to listen to your personal conversations, they often do. Be careful what you say and who you're saying it to. It's a very big mistake to discuss the protruding waist of sound operator number two. This can result in your mic being muted, your song being cut, and premature death.

So basically – be nice, be tidy, be careful what you say, and always smile at important people. Follow these rules, and you will never have a problem backstage.

Actors – if you are in a show that you hate, think of the money. Failing that, think of the credit. Failing that, think of the pub, dear.

Keeping It Fresh

The term 'keep it fresh' haunts actors from the second they are born until the moment they do their last small-scale tour. As an actor, when you sign the contract my PA sends you, you are legally obliged to keep your performance 'fresh' and 'new' during every single performance. This is very easy for the resident director to say in a notes session – but the resident director is not the person who has to perform eight shows a week. Invariably, acting can, like any other job, become tiresome, monotonous and boring. After all, you are being paid to say the same lines and move the same way night after night after night. Hamlet said 'words, words, words' – and that is exactly what dialogue feels like after six months of saying it on a daily basis.

So you auditioned, got the job, rehearsed, had your opening night, and are now in week four of a fifteen-month run. And already you are *bored*! This is inevitable, particularly if you stand at the back dressed as a guard with one line of dialogue. After eight performances even a theatrical genius like Les Dennis would get bored. Many tutors say there are numerous ways to keep a performance fresh – ranging from saying the lines differently, using a different energy, a different intention, and sucking on a sweet. But in truth, every actor gets bored of a show. There is only so much you can do, particularly if you only have one line – and on the one occasion when you alter it slightly you get told off by the company manager for looking like you're having an epileptic fit.

One of the best ways of keeping your performance fresh is the 'no-pants technique'. This is a remarkable little secret that Shakespeare wrote about in *Hamlet*: 'O, that this too too solid flesh would melt, thaw and resolve itself into a dew!' – the 'flesh' being Hamlet's Y-fronts. The no-pants method works on many levels. Firstly, it keeps your pants fresh. Secondly, it allows easy access to your naughty region. But most importantly – it will give you a little 'secret', which makes you more watchable on stage.

This no-pants technique has another name in the industry: charisma. Many actors are described as having charisma – that indefinable magnetism which makes someone very watchable – but it is simply because they aren't wearing any underwear. They know it, the audience subconsciously knows it, and the wardrobe mistress definitely knows it. Try it yourself – the next time you're doing something boring and repetitious, slip off your pants and see what happens.

My casting director used this method regularly during auditions in the eighties, but he was rather naughty – in fact, he didn't wear *anything* from his waist down. This was fine until he stood up during the boys' recalls for *Oliver!* Bless. Some of those kids have never been the same since, dear.

Actor friends have informed me that the no-pants technique is also very useful when you're feeling nervous about auditions. However, when using it for this reason you reverse it – and imagine that the audition panel are the ones without underwear. In fact, one of my friends always finds it useful to imagine that the panel are completely naked. It apparently gives him a rather empowering sensation – particularly when he imagines their kinky parts are all petite and mangled (mine are neither petite *or* mangled, I might add, dear).

Boredom Games

I often talk to actors when they are in after-show detention about why they decided to be naughty. The most common answer is because they were bored. I have also learnt from these same actors that they play games on stage to relieve their boredom. Of course, I am not a fan of actors playing games of any sort on stage, but since I want to cover all areas in this book I feel I should include them – as they are rather amusing.

Obviously, I never want actors in my shows to partake in any of the games listed below. However, if you're in a show produced by Kenwright or Lloyd Webber then feel free.

Pass the Button

I'm told this game is very easy to participate in – and is frequently used by members of the RSC – particularly during the History Plays (the long and dull ones). One member of the cast holds a button – or similar small object – on stage and passes it to someone else in the company. The button has to be accepted by the actor who is 'tagged' with it, and then that person holding it must pass it on. If you have the button at the end of Act One you have to buy crisps and salty snacks in the pub afterwards. If you possess it at the end of the second half you have to buy the first round of drinks. If you possess the button at the end of the show for more than three consecutive nights you have to donate your entire week's wages to the ASM.

As you get braver with this game, the size of the object you pass around increases, until it is too obvious and becomes distracting to the audience. I remember seeing a production of *Macbeth* where the cast were passing a blow-up doll to each other. It was fine until it got stuck on the end of Macduff's sword, popped, and ended up straddling Macbeth's decapitated head. Luckily most of the audience thought it was part of the action as the doll bore a striking resemblance to the actress playing Lady Macbeth.

Getting Ready at the Last Possible Minute

As you settle into the run you will find the routine of getting into costume a lot easier. Another little game that has been reported to me is 'getting ready at the last possible minute' – i.e. after the five-minute call (which is very naughty indeed). Obviously, if your role requires the application of huge prosthetics you should start getting ready at the quarter, but if it's just a costume, parting of the hair and simple make-up, then apparently you must attempt it at the five. The worst thing that can happen is you make the show go up late, and get an official warning. But I wouldn't worry about that. Official warnings don't mean anything anyway. It's the unofficial ones you have to worry about, dear (particularly when working for me).

Gurning Upstage

Pretty self-explanatory.

A word of warning: Whilst I understand these games are only a bit of fun, they are only fun if you are doing them for other producers. If I ever hear of you playing them whilst in any of my shows you will be disciplined in actors' detention, and be forced to go back to Year One at Sylvia Young Theatre School, dear.

Long day ahead? Play the jazz-hands game. Do as many cheeky jazz hands during normal conversation as you can without anyone noticing, dear.

Actors' Detention

I have noticed something quite disturbing happening to actors. Every year they seem to get naughtier, bolder and more creative than the year before. And this worries me – as it is not the actor's job. An actor, by trade, is legally only enti-tled to do what the producer and director tells them, and not impose their own ideas on anything. When they do, it com-plicates things, and directors and casting departments get nervous. An actor is there to do what they are told – not to talk back to those who have told them.

Because of this, and as a result of horrific things I have read on show reports, actors' detention gets busier every week. Actors' detention is something I was forced to invent when an overeager performer continually thought it appropriate to get his penis out during the curtain call. I don't know what possessed him, particularly as he was playing Daddy Warbucks in *Annie*. It was truly shocking. As a result I made this actor go to detention every week so he could learn right from wrong. It was only after the fifth week of writing ten thousand lines of 'I will not get my penis out in the curtain call' that he finally understood. And then he started getting his bum out instead. In retrospect, I knew I shouldn't have employed someone who had just finished three years in *Chicago*. The casts of that show are always far too eager to get their bits out.

Actors' detention is not just a clever way of allowing me to whip actors (although this *is* a bonus) – it is incredibly important for actors to relearn the discipline they originally had when entering the business. Detention happens straight after a mid-week performance and takes place in the green room where desks, chairs and a blackboard have been set out. My casting director now insists on taking these sessions, as he is marvellous at awarding discipline when and where it is needed. He also gets deep thrills dressing up as a schoolteacher and fiddling with his cane.

The detentions themselves consist of lines written in silence, theatrical mathematical equations and *Crystal Maze*-style challenges. Some of these challenges are very tough, both physically and mentally – so tough, in fact, that we sadly lost one actor during the process (but he had a good understudy so it didn't really matter). However, the biggest and most terrifying challenge in actors' detention is not being allowed to talk. And more specifically, not being allowed to talk about *yourself*.

This final challenge has crushed many a well-known actor. It is very startling to witness, because 'talking about yourself' is something which is second nature to every actor. When you put two performers in a room their natural inclination is to chat about themselves and the business. Sometimes they will try and break the pattern by asking the other person lots of questions first – but these questions will inevitably be about upcoming auditions and who their agent is, which will naturally lead to them talking about their *own* agent. And *bang*! They're talking about themselves again. It really is very difficult, and is something of an addiction for actors worldwide. It is a well-known fact that farmers like to talk about sheep, butchers about meat, and actors about themselves.

....

Actors – it really isn't necessary to use 'The Method' when playing an Oompa Loompa, dear.

....

'Touch an Actor' Scheme

Famous actors these days are treated like gods and praised for their performances on and off stage. I think it's time the general public learnt that they are like you and me – and are given the chance to touch them. It is a scheme I have been trying to get approved by various acting organisations over the years – but for some reason there has always been considerable apprehension.

What I propose is that actors in any company offer themselves to be touched by members of the public – for a fee. I hear actors complaining about their awful wages on a daily basis, so I think this simple activity would provide a solution for all parties. I am not suggesting that every actor would be keen on the idea, but I know many who would gratefully be touched for cash.

The 'Touch an Actor' scheme would have different rates for different body parts. For example, a few little taps on the head would cost you a tenner, but a good cupping of the balls would cost at least £30 – depending on the size of the balls in question. But, of course, it all depends on how far the actor wants to go.

In the seventeenth and eighteenth centuries anyone could pay a few shillings to go backstage and watch actors getting dressed and undressed. They didn't even have to be watching the show. The backstage antics were just as much of a show as the onstage ones.

Anyhow, it's an idea I want to trial very soon – so if any actors out there would like to offer their body for touching purposes please let me know. And for you, lucky reader, please see the back of this book for your special 'Touch an Actor' voucher.

If in doubt, fade to black.

Different Types of Performance

Physical Theatre

Physical theatre is a mysterious art form that was created in the early twentieth century by a group of actors who found talking and moving at the same time far too taxing – so they developed a technique using deep lunges, star jumps and standing on their tiptoes. It was a fascinating visual feast that allowed actors to experiment in unknown territories – bending, stretching and utilising every part of their body in a physical way. If only they knew they were paving the way for *Puppetry of the Penis*, dear.

Many actors believe that there is no difference between normal theatre and physical theatre – that, in fact, to be a good actor in the first place you have to be physical. Of course, I see their point – and most actors will perform with a certain degree of physicality – but performers these days frequently feel compelled to adopt the hugely unsatisfactory 'standing still and talking' stance. Whilst there is nothing wrong with this technique, I find it rather unimpressive and repetitious. I don't just want to see people talking on stage, I want to be entertained! If I merely wanted to see people standing and talking I would go and book a season ticket for the Royal Court.

I must admit to feeling sorry for these 'standing still' actors – as I'm sure they're suppressing an inherent yearn to release their inner jazz hands. I don't blame the actor for this, it's not their fault – I blame the actor-training. Many schools these days are not jazz-hand fans, and whip this natural inclination out of the young, enthusiastic performer. I think it scandalous, I really do. There is nothing wrong with the use of jazz hands – they provide a relief, a celebration, and their significant use is a symbol of theatre throughout the world. Just look at Laurence Olivier. Apparently his whole technique was based on the jazz-hand method. He was just very sparing in his use of it.

Many of our most famous theatre companies have their own distinctive physical styles as described below:

Royal Shakespeare Company – A very earthy, flat-footed physicality that involves standing still for long periods – particularly when holding a spear.

National Theatre – A physicality that uses expressive, gurning faces and bold arm gestures. If you give certain members of the company a luminous jacket they become highly skilled at landing aircrafts.

Donmar Warehouse – A light-footed, subtle physicality, with a preference to using frequent head movements.

Royal Court Theatre – A physicality that involves constantly looking at the floor – helping to imply harrowed, tortured characters.

Physical-theatre performers tend to have a great facility in allowing their body to encapsulate a character totally. Whether it be using mime, mask work, dance, or solely movement, their performances come from a more physical understanding and appreciation of the character and story. Not to say that the physical-theatre performer never offers a cerebral performance – because indeed they do – but what is offered is more a study of the physical attributes of human nature.

Of course, physical theatre does not dissociate itself from dialogue – in fact, many companies use the combination of text and bold physicality to aid their telling of the story. One of the foremost practitioners of physical theatre in the UK is Steven Berkoff. He was celebrated for his version of Kafka's *Metamorphosis*, and his plays *East* and *West*. Berkoff (or 'Jerkoff' to his friends) is an expert in the difficult techniques of physical theatre – he gurns, shouts, jumps, makes big arm gestures, grinds his teeth, lunges and spits the length of a football pitch. In fact, it was because of Steven that 'splash' seats were invented – as the first four rows of his audience would always get splattered with spittle. Fine if you're into that sort of thing, but terrible if you're not partial to a bit of dribble.

I have witnessed many physical-theatre rehearsals in my time, and one thing I have observed is that they always contain a lot more physical contact than other forms of theatre. Whether this contact is hugging, slapping, caressing, lifting, or simply playing with the other person's balls – it is always very present and vital in physical theatre. And I wonder if that is why actors want to get involved in it. I'm sure the prospect of pressing other performer's bottoms and breasts in a purely 'artistic' way is marvellous – as every touch is justified as being a carefully controlled and planned piece of performance art. My casting director is a big fan of physical theatre, and actually offers one-on-one masterclasses at his house. I've no idea what it involves but I wouldn't recommend going unless you enjoy wrestling with an old queen.

There are many institutions that offer training in the art of physical theatre – one of the most well known is a school in Paris called Lecoq, founded by Jacques Lecoq in 1956. It is known by many for its strict disciplines, '7 states of tension' work, and 'creative collaboration' philosophy. It is also known worldwide for having a name that sounds like a part of the male anatomy. I am sure many people apply to the school thinking they will spend two years studying men's private parts. I certainly did – but sadly I didn't get offered a place.

In fact, I used to be very dear friends with a physical-theatre teacher from Paris, who moved to London in the seventies to continue and develop his teaching. He originally worked freelance at a lot of the top drama schools of the time. But one of the things that differentiated him from other similar teachers was that he believed the challenge of physical theatre was not actually to get too physical with the other performers. He said the key to physical theatre was 'choosing when to be physical'. Unfortunately, many actors today choose to be physical far too early and far too often. And it usually happens in their digs in week one of the tour.

Many performers get confused about whether they are actually performing in a physical-theatre piece. The most reliable way to confirm this is if your naughty bits hurt after the performance. If they do, then you are.

To succeed in physical theatre you have to have a firm bottom, a large appendage, a good jockstrap, a face that looks good in masks, and a passion for throwing short actors around the stage.

Christmas Eve: the day when a great theatrical tradition lives in every theatre across the land. 'The speed-run', dear.

Pantomime

Once a year a great theatrical tradition is practised in most theatres around the country. It is an event that has been passed down from father to child, from mother to milkman, from cross-dresser to giant. It is a marvellous, magical time when theatres actually make money. It is, of course, the Christmas pantomime.

Pantomimes are a hugely important event in a theatre's diary. They are the show that sells far more than any other, and in many instances it is the success of the panto that allows the theatre to survive for the rest of the year.

Sadly, many people in the business look down on panto as an inferior form of theatre. It is not in the slightest. These people have just not seen a good one, or don't really understand the joy of pantomime. Most people's first venture into a theatre is to see a panto with their family at Christmas. Children have a wonderful time, and leave the theatre amazed by all the colours, effects and good honest fun – unless the panto has got Jim Davidson in it. In which case the child is put off theatre for life.

A panto is steeped in tradition and derived from the Italian style of theatre called *Commedia dell'Arte* – which was popularised in Britain when Christopher Biggins and Danny La Rue got carried away dressed as French sailors at Soho fetish clubs in the sixties.

A modern panto has many expectations – one of the most important being the promise of a huge celebrity. Of course, in today's climate the word 'celebrity' is used in the loosest sense possible. In reality, for producers it is far more important to have a familiar TV face in their panto than a 'nobody'. The simple reason for this is that it is much easier to fill an auditorium night after night after night with a 'name' – even if that name has no talent at all. You see, when a producer pays for a name we are not just buying the performance, we are also buying all the publicity that automatically comes with it. For instance, if we get someone who has just been on *Big Brother*, all the local press are interested, local radio stations will do interviews, and local TV shows will be keen to have them on the sofa. With an unknown it is very difficult even getting a little write-up in the local gazette. Which is a sad state of affairs – but when I get criticised for employing celebrities I have to remind everyone that I am trying to make money. I don't do it entirely for pleasure. Theatre, TV and radio are all types of showbusiness. And that's something you should always bear in mind: it's called show*business*, dear.

Actors should always remember they are working in a business. It is marvellous that some actors are enthusiastic, dedicated and willing to work for nothing, but they have to realise they are always working for someone else – and that someone else is always trying to make money. Whether that money be instantaneous, or whether the show is primarily about promoting someone's reputation, it is a business. There is no point being bitter about the fact that celebrities or reality stars get the job – it is because they help sell the product. And the show is the product. And this is particularly true in a pantomime.

There are many rules in panto that can make the whole process a lot easier. One of the most important is to be nice to the celebrities, even if they are terrible. I understand how frustrating it is for actors and dancers who are on £500 a week when the celebrity is on £30,000. The usual panto celebrity will not have done much theatre work and will spend most of the rehearsal process trying to figure out how to say their lines. This requires patience from more experienced members of the company, who are sometimes required to assist them in their learning process. Many times I have witnessed dancers telling the celebrity how to open and close their mouth on cue. And still the celebrity gets confused and ends up dribbling all over the kids from the local dance school.

A good friend of mine is a panto producer, and has become a millionaire from his success. He is very clever when dealing with celebrities and in particular their wages – and can substantially knock down a celeb's wage depending on the media coverage they've had that year. For example, if a celeb has recently been on *I'm a Celebrity Get Me Out of Here*, their 'bums on seats' value hugely increases and consequently they demand a higher wage. However, if they've been in the press for having sex with strangers in public places then their 'bums on seats' value decreases – so he is able to knock five or six grand off, dear.

If you are ever in the unfortunate position of being told by a celebrity that they 'do the funnies' (make the jokes), you are in for a tough time. This doesn't really happen now with new-style comedians – it is something that 'old-school' actors and comedians tend to do. Their aim is simply to scare you, and establish their status. They are the stars. It is their name on the posters. People are in the audience to see them – so how dare you be better! It really is infuriating when this happens, but whenever I've had complaints from younger actors I just tell them to accept it and get on with it. There is nothing worse than a star who doesn't feel like the star.

I remember one case where a certain actress was aware that a fellow actor was getting more laughs than her. So during one performance she had her husband sit in the audience with a copy of the script and make notes on when the other actor got the laughs. The following night she changed the delivery of all her lines so that she got all the laughs, leaving the other actor looking like an embarrassing amateur. Naughty.

A panto is one of the hardest acting jobs it is possible to do. It will often involve more than twenty shows a week, living in the theatre, and cross-dressing on a daily basis. This can be a heavy burden on your voice, your physical stamina and your sex life. Many actors find that, after performing twenty shows a week, the last thing they want to do is an extra performance in bed. In fact, the best example of 'suffering for your art' is a pantomime at 10 a.m., dear.

Your time in a panto depends entirely on what the rest of the cast are like. Usually a panto cast are lovely and will just get straight on with the job as the rehearsal period is so short. Most pantomimes will rehearse for one or two weeks – unless it is a panto for the RSC or Old Vic – in which case you will start rehearsing in March. Many people think eight months is far too long to rehearse a panto, but anyone who witnessed Ian McKellen's Sarah the Cook at the Old Vic will tell you it was the most moving performance ever seen on a London stage.

Never trust a Buttons who is over the age of thirty-five. Many older actors who first played Buttons when they were eighteen are now still playing him at the age of sixty – which makes no sense whatsoever. It is very uncomfortable when the OAP Buttons tells the twenty-two-year-old Cinderella that he loves her. Unless, of course, the panto is being produced by the BBC – where this kind of thing is normal, dear.

When playing Snow White, never be fooled by your seven dwarfs. I have heard countless stories where the dwarfs convinced Snow White that she should sleep with them so they could all be truly close and comfortable. Never, ever do this. Unless you want to witness Grumpy feeling Happy.

Another ingredient of a successful panto are the 'babes'. To be honest, I find the term 'babes' a little wrong, as the 'babes' are the young children who are brought in from the local dance school, and not the women who work in the local strip joint. I always feel uneasy calling these kids 'babe' and instead I call them the 'little dears'. This term is useful, as it sounds both affectionate and condescending all at the same time. Whenever the 'little dears' are in or around the theatre they will be followed by some large ladies who have an abundance of facial hair. These are the kids' chaperones. These ladies (and men) have the difficult task of keeping an eye on the children at all times and making sure no one goes within two metres of them. Naturally, it is very important that these children are protected and cared for in the theatre – particularly when there are men dressed as women, women dressed as men, and people called Dick. And because of this, the chaperone has to remind the children constantly that they are in a theatre – and it is not real life. They also have the important job of making sure that the adults keep their distance – and it is usual that in order to speak to the 'little dears' you have to send a letter, get it approved, be CRB-checked, sanitise your hands, go in front of the local council, and promise not to talk about burgers, chips or One Direction.

When Abanazar bonks Widow Twankey – it's called 'awankey', dear.

A hugely important tradition at Christmas time is Secret Santa – where every member of the company buys a present for someone else anonymously. It is a lovely festive game that reveals what everyone thinks about their colleagues. There is usually a budget set of around £5 – although sometimes people spend a lot more or a lot less. People who spend less are the cheapskates of the company, and people who spend more are the show-offs. But, of course, if you are the lead in the show, you are legally obliged to spend at least three times the set amount.

The aim of Secret Santa is to offend as many people as possible. This can be done by buying inappropriate gifts, cheap gifts, or gifts that you were given the year before. I have seen many companies reduced to tears as a result of the Secret Santa gifts. It really is quite funny, and something which I always aim to witness. There are no real rules to it either – apart from making sure that everyone gets a present. There is nothing worse than a gift-less performer screaming and sobbing in the corner.

In approximately the second week of January most pantomimes finish – and many tired, withered, alcohol-sodden actors head back home. It is a sad time when frocks are hung up, greasepaint is packed away, and gurning is forgotten about for nine months. If you ever see one of these ex-panto actors wandering the streets, please do your bit and buy them a biscuit, a cake, or simply give them a smile. It's not easy being an actor. And it's even less easy being an unemployed actor in January.

Actors resign themselves to the fact that they won't get any auditions during January – as this is the time when casting directors and directors sit at home watching DVD box sets whilst playing with themsleves. And why not? We all need to do that once in a while.

When actors finish a show, in this case a panto, it can be very hard returning to normal life. Particularly after you've been busting your gut for three months entertaining families across the country. Suddenly coming back to nothing can be very disheartening indeed, and is, in many respects, the hardest part of being an actor. I have seen it first hand, when ex-partners of mine took weeks to get over their post-show depression. And that is what it is – a form of depression, as you attempt to move on from the life you have been living.

I am always upset when I see unemployed friends of mine wandering aimlessly around London at the start of a new year. It saddens me deeply, so I do my bit and buy them a sausage roll. Actors love a bit of cheap meat in flaky pastry, dear.

....

An 'unpaid opportunity' tends only to be an opportunity for the people offering the opportunity, dear.

....

Fringe Theatre

Whilst it is not good for the bank balance, sometimes a fringe-theatre job can be a brilliant way of marketing yourself and showing yourself in a different light. I have been to many fringe shows recently and have been bowled over by the excellent performances and wonderful production values.

It used to be presumed that a fringe show would be second-rate, and performed by a company of inebriated amateurs. I remember many awkward evenings being bribed to accompany an agent to see their clients perform in what can only be described as a converted toilet at the back of a mouldy public house. Whilst there is nothing wrong with converted toilets, they are not generally the most accessible of surroundings to turn into an adequate theatre space. However, I am pleased to report that many fringe venues these days pride themselves on producing shows equal in standard to the West End – and in some circumstances even better.

The problem that has always faced fringe venues is the reluctance of people to pay £15 to £25 to see a show in a small, cold theatre when they can pay the same money for a seat in a West End one (albeit a seat in the upper circle with a pillar in front of them). Also it used to be that the lure of 'names' in West End theatres made them far more desirable.

However, things are changing, and even 'names' now embrace the joy and creativity of appearing in these smaller, more intimate spaces.

London has a host of marvellous fringe venues – the Union, King's Head, Southwark Playhouse, Jermyn Street and Finborough, to name but a few. I always admire and applaud those actors and company members who dedicate so much of their time – often for no fee – to create this kind of theatre. The joy of fringe theatre is that the space is so intimate you can almost smell the actors. This is not always a good thing, particularly in the second half of a sweaty musical, but the fact that the actors are so close means they have no way of hiding. They are performing inches in front of you – which is thrilling.

There are some people who find this intimacy rather intimidating. At the other end of the scale there are people who find it a little *too* thrilling. There was a man in the early eighties who used to go to all fringe shows in a large mac. His hand would disappear in his coat as soon as any beautiful actors walked on stage and he'd start fiddling around under there. Of course, we all presumed Michael Billington was just writing notes about the show, but on the one occasion I sat next to him I wondered if he was doing something else. I don't know. Anyhow, he's a very nice man, so we never talk about that, dear.

Many fringe venues have a flexibility that some of the larger theatres do not have, so they can support and nurture new writing. Some bigger venues do their bit and offer courses and workshops – but because of the huge financial risk involved in putting on new work, it is often deemed far too risky. This is where fringe theatre comes into its own. Whilst fringe venues themselves are not cheap to hire – with running costs, marketing and staff to pay for – they can provide the perfect platform for new work. And recently, as a result, some of this new work has transferred to bigger West End theatres – proving fringe theatre to be a marvellous launch pad for emerging artists.

I am not a fan of anyone having to work for free – although it is rather useful for my bank balance. Some of my dear actor friends tell me it is hard enough for artists to make a decent living on Equity minimum, and virtually impossible when working for nothing. Some companies offer travel expenses, and others offer a share of the profit. However, it is very rare that a show in the West End, let alone a fringe venue, makes much of a profit – unless you are lucky enough to produce a real winner. It is a sad fact that most profit-share shows don't actually have any profit to share. Most of the time a show will just cover costs – which is very tough on the actors and technical team who offer their services for nothing. It is a very difficult position, as actors wish to look like they are working – and sometimes simply want to stretch their acting muscles. They also see fringe theatre as a super opportunity to perform roles that they would otherwise not have the chance to do. In truth, the only way that this will change is if everyone stopped working for nothing. It would demand a total change of culture, attitude and value in our industry. We can but hope.

....

Actors – remember: no one actually knows what they're doing. So keep pretending. Eventually you'll make everyone believe that you do, dear.

....

A QUICK SCENE CHANGE
IN THE MIDDLE OF ACT THREE:

TOURING

OR
PERFORMING ON THE ROAD

I used to be a tour de force. Now I'm just forced to tour.

Touring

I have known many actors who have set off on tour and are never heard of again. They have got lost in the twilight zone of theatre digs and regional theatre green rooms. So whether you are performing in a Theatre in Education tour of *Lord of the Rings*, or a number-one tour of *Fifty Shades of Grey: The Musical*, learning how to survive on tour is vitally important.

A Concise Guide to Types of Touring

Rural touring – This usually involves touring to village halls, small arts venues and farmers' bedrooms. Actors often complain of feeling isolated on rural tours – and say conditions on the road can be very hazardous. Whilst this may be true, there are also benefits. For example, you can learn how to milk cows and feed pigs, which is perfect experience for future *Emmerdale* auditions.

Theatre in Education (TIE) – This type of touring usually means you'll be performing in school halls and sixth-form drama studios. On special occasions you may even be asked to perform for the headmaster, in his office, alone. This type of performance is slightly different and involves the use of a cane – but can be very rewarding financially. When doing TIE tours the type of show varies dramatically depending on the target audience, but usually you will be dealing with subjects on the National Curriculum. In primary schools, 'Drug and Substance Abuse' is a particular favourite; and in secondary schools 'Going on the Dole' always seems beneficial. Personally, I think Theatre in Education is a marvellous resource for schools – and in many instances is the first time youngsters experience real live theatre. Recently I was lucky enough to witness a nursery schools' tour of *The Vagina Monologues*. It was really rather moving to see the impact it had on all those toddlers.

A national tour – This means you'll be touring to theatres around the country. Sometimes you can be at each theatre for a week, sometimes a month, sometimes three months, and sometimes several years. An actor I know started touring *Dreamboats and Petticoats* three years ago, and is now contractually obliged to stay in it for the rest of his life. He keeps reminding me that 'at least it's work'. I keep reminding him that it's *Dreamboats and Petticoats*.

National tours can be a lot of fun, and allow you to discover, explore and copulate in many of the most exciting and historical theatres in the UK. Some theatres are big, some are small and some are just medium. But, of course, it's not the size of the theatre, it's what you do with them that counts. When travelling to these theatres you will often get the chance to meet and befriend some of the strangest creatures on the planet: the resident stage crew. These people are invariably very nice and, just like the theatres they work in, come in all different shapes and sizes. There are fly-men, spotlight operators, stage managers, crew, master carpenters and stage-door keepers. Each one of them will have their own hiding place in the theatre – and many of them never actually leave the building. You should always try and get on their good side by giving them Carlsberg, Fosters and, most importantly, Special Brew.

I would do anything for love, but I won't do TIE.

Before a tour begins, you will invariably be given a 'digs list'. Every regional theatre has a digs list. The digs list is meant to contain information about the accommodation that is available for each theatre. In truth, the digs list tends to be just names and addresses of horny old ladies who want to show you their panty collection. In fact, an easy way to bypass the theatre digs list altogether is by purchasing a local copy of *Readers' Wives*.

When booking digs I advise you to find somewhere close to the theatre. This avoids long walks and arduous bus journeys – and makes drunken staggers home easier. There is nothing worse than getting drunk in the morning and having to walk half an hour to the theatre for your matinee.

When arriving at your digs for the first time you should make sure your room has a bed. I have heard countless stories where actors have turned up to their digs only to discover that the room they are staying in is, in fact, a hallway, outhouse or shed. I even heard of one actor that stayed in a toilet for a week in Scarborough. But apparently Martin Shaw paid extra for that.

Some actors even like to share digs with fellow cast members. This can be a clever way of saving money. If you get on with your fellow cast then there is no reason why this shouldn't work. But there are things you have to be prepared for. Many actors 'change' when in different surroundings –

particularly in the early hours of the morning. I remember a spate of sightings in Cornwall that made the national news – where people thought there was a beast on Bodmin Moor. It was, in actual fact, just Brian Blessed on all fours after a particularly heavy night.

Saving money on tour can be very difficult, even if you are lucky enough to be on Equity minimum. Many actors find that they are forced to pay double rent – for both their home as well as their digs on tour. Some people deal with this by subletting their home to other actors. But always do your background checks first. You don't want someone staying in your room who only did a one-year drama course.

Also, 'eating out' can become an expensive habit on tour – albeit a tasty one. At any one time there are thousands of starving actors touring the UK – and you can usually find them convening on a daily basis in some of the countries most well-established and critically celebrated restaurants. Wetherspoon's is a particular favourite, dear.

It is very easy to fall into the habit of going to the pub every night after your show. Whilst this is a very sociable way of relaxing, after a few weeks you will realise that you are spending your entire wage on beer, salty snacks and quiz machines. And then there's the coffee. An actor is legally obliged to turn up to rehearsals with a cup of coffee. So, if on average an actor drinks two cups of 'bought' coffee a day – amounting to around £5 – then a rehearsal week of six days is £30 – and a monthly spend is at least £120. If you are doing a one-year contract that amounts to nearly £1,440 on *just* coffee. Which could be your tax bill for the year!

....

When a touring show is advertised as 'direct from the West End' it usually means it did a two-week run at the Charing Cross Theatre, dear.

....

Eating on Tour

I always advise actors to take multivitamins with them on tour, along with a selection of fruit and vegetables. You have to protect your immune system – particularly when tech week is upon you. Tech weeks are exhausting experiences, and your successful completion of them cannot rely solely on alcohol and cigarettes. Over the years I have lost many a good actor during tech week, mainly due to a bad diet, an increased amount of alcohol, and a lack of respect for the stage crew.

Sometimes you may be extremely lucky and your landlady will offer to cook for you, which can be very nice. However, it can also be very un-nice if your landlady is a sweaty mammoth who has a tendency to dribble and pick at her feet. I know many actors who have eaten home-cooked food which contained scabs, hair and body parts. Although you may feel rude turning this home-prepared delicacy down, your gut will thank you for it in the long run.

A great treat on tour is the 'microwave meal'. These handy little snacks are a lifesaver, especially nowadays when you can get *healthy* microwave meals. M&S is a particular favourite – they do a lovely range of healthy meals that fill you up and take less than an hour to come out the other end. You should always make 'microwave hunting' one of your first priorities when entering a new theatre. It is also very handy to find a fridge. The fridge comes in very useful, particularly for keeping your interval alcohol chilled. It is also a rather fun place to hide the understudies in.

Actors – becoming a vegan does not make you a better actor. It just makes you a smellier one, dear.

A recent trend in actors is to become a vegan. Whilst this is all lovely, and may have long-term health benefits, it is not very considerate to your fellow cast members. There is nothing worse than walking on stage to be greeted with the pungent aroma of a vegan's fart. I have had the pleasure of sitting in a rehearsal room watching an entirely vegan cast rehearse the dance routine to 'The American Dream'. And I can tell you, I will never forget the smell of those fourteen bendy vegans doing the splits.

I am not saying that I don't approve of healthy eating, because of course I do. But I think everything should be done in moderation. I tried being a vegan once for a month, and whilst I lost half a stone in body weight and felt fantastically fit, my partner banished me to the spare room as the things that were coming out of my bottom were toxic.

Of course, in rehearsals I will always try and provide biscuits. Biscuits are a necessity in the rehearsal room – and a lack of them can cause extreme unpleasantness. I remember Brian Blessed getting so upset about the lack of biscuits one morning that he ran away, left the show, and started doing voice-overs for *Peppa Pig*.

Sometimes, if you are extra lucky, cake will be given – to keep you keen. With cake I always get my company manager to report back who takes the biggest slice – as it is useful to know who the greedy actors are. I even know one director who begins his rehearsal period by throwing a tin of Quality Streets on the floor and telling the actors to 'find their favourite'. He finds the whole exercise very revealing, and believes that each sweet says something different about the actor. If ever you find yourself faced with this 'sweetie challenge', be warned: do not choose the Purple One. And never, ever take two sweets, as this means you hog centre-stage, dear.

Essential Things to Take on Tour

A pillow – Avoids you resting your head on a sweaty, lumpy one. There is nothing quite so disconcerting as being confined to two months of sleeping on a stain-covered brick.

DVD box set – You need something to keep you entertained when going back to your cold, Dickensian digs. Even if you are sharing digs it can be rather fun to have a DVD night with your room-mates. It alleviates boredom and is a welcome distraction when you have nothing else to say to each other.

Warm pyjamas – Inevitably you will get cold, particularly when touring in the winter. It is highly recommended you have something warm and comfortable to snuggle into on those occasions. Your pyjamas do not necessarily have to be sexy and flattering, unless you plan on using another member of the company to keep you warm. If this is the case, may I recommend a larger member of the company as they tend to have more naturally occurring body heat.

Personally, I always pack my themed pyjamas. If I'm going to have an overnight stay watching *Les Mis* somewhere, I'll take my *Les Mis* pyjamas. They are tight, beardy, and have a life-long 'One Day More' guarantee.

Emergency card – You should always carry an emergency contact card in your wallet. This card should have your agent's phone number and your headshot on it. It proves very useful if you ever get so hideously drunk that you forget who you are represented by. I have heard of actors losing out on potential roles due to forgetting who their agent is. At some point in your career you will undoubtedly be found outside some public toilets by an important casting director – and in moments like this it is essential you are prepared and have your emergency card at hand.

Cutlery – A clean set of your own personal cutlery can be a godsend. I always carry some with me – particularly when dining at colleagues' houses. Nothing is more off-putting than a knife with old pickle residue, or a fork with fungus growing between the prongs. Most theatres will have some cutlery, but you have to be careful. A lot of the cutlery in theatres dates back to the early seventeenth century – and indeed some recent tests done on a spoon found backstage at the Palladium had some of Shakespeare's saliva on it. Sadly this was quickly sucked off by an overambitious understudy. However, there will undoubtedly be theatres that don't have cutlery – and if you are equipped with your own you will be greatly admired and envied by the rest of the company.

A cup – Many theatres will have a lack of cups, and any that you can find will usually belong to the resident stage crew. *Be warned*: never, ever steal a cup that belongs to the stage-management team. It can have disastrous results. Stage management are a very important species who are essential in the smooth running of a show. If they are ever starved of a relaxing drink from their favourite cup they will strike, refuse to move the set, or simply drop the safety curtain halfway through your lovely monologue. There have even been extreme cases where actors have gone to their dressing room and found naughty pictures of the human anatomy scribbled all over their headshots. Shocking, dear.

I suggest having a neutral cup, of average size and not very expensive. Use a marker pen to write your name very clearly on *all* sides – and also stick a copy of your headshot on the bottom, so those actors who can't read have no excuse.

You should resist the natural urge to take a 'show mug' on tour with you – as this is a sure way to provoke ridicule and taunting for the rest of the contract.

A good book – Reading matter is particularly essential if you spend a lot of time offstage during the show. In which case you may need a few good books. If you can't read, there are some wonderful animated books that you can just stare at instead.

A small, medium or large bag – The size of your bag varies on the length of the tour. But the use of the bag is for the same reason: to put all your receipts in. *Always* ask for a receipt for everything and anything you buy and do on tour. You will need them when sorting expenses for your tax return. Never throw a receipt away, even if it's for an embarrassing porno movie you bought in Hull, as this can still be classed as 'career research'.

Make-up bag – Every good actor has a make-up bag. And every really good actor has two. Having a good supply of make-up is very useful – even if you are in a show where the director tells you not to wear it. Directors are funny like that. These days they tend to want things to look realistic, which results in a plethora of pasty-looking actors skulking around our stages. It is absurd! If I wanted to watch a lot of grey, depressed humans shuffling about I would go to my local dole office. When I go to the theatre I want to be entertained, uplifted, enlightened – and for that I want to see rouge, nail varnish and fake eyelashes. I don't care if it's not historically accurate. It's not historically accurate that trains can sing, but did that stop Andrew Lloyd Webber? No. I rest my case.

Your script – You should always have a copy of the script with you – or at least in your dressing room. It gives the impression you take your job very seriously indeed. If you really want to impress, have some of those sticky coloured things randomly sticking out, and write something on every page.

Your contract – There will be times when you get into a disagreement with your company manager about overtime, hours worked, subsistence money, etc. It saves a lot of unnecessary time and energy if you have your contract to hand. Although, to be honest, your contract really doesn't mean much. But it is a rather intimidating and clever tool to bring out during a company meeting.

....

An actor without a contract is the same as an actor with a contract, dear.

....

Your favourite musical – Always have a copy of your favourite musical with you. Whether it is on your iPod, your laptop, or simply on a CD, it is an essential companion for long and arduous journeys between venues. Your favourite musical will hopefully have good memories for you – and is the perfect enthusiasm restorer for when you are feeling down (unless you are listening to *Love Never Dies*).

Glasses – Useful for reading books and watching TV (depending on your eyesight). And also a necessary tool if you are unsure about your character. If in doubt, give them a pair of glasses.

A shirt and shoes – Always take at least one nice pair of shoes and a good shirt/dress with you. This is for the press night – when you dress to impress. Some actors like to 'dress down' on these occasions as they think it makes them appear cool. It does not. It just makes them look like they can't be bothered. My dears, if you can't be bothered to dress nicely then don't bother coming. You are an actor – and an actor should always dress like an actor, particularly at social events.

Trainers and warm-up gear – Vital for the company warm-up. Also useful for going to the gym. Many theatres will have special discounts for touring companies at local leisure centres. These gyms can be very cheap, and are a marvellous way of getting rid of excess alcohol weight, and picking up discreet encounters.

A sleeping bag – Essential for when the bed you are offered on tour is covered in other actors' stains. There is nothing as off-putting as a dirty bed, and the quick laying of your own sleeping bag alters this situation in a second. It will also act as a brilliant extra cover if the bed you are staying in is too cold. A good sleeping bag can also be used to hide bottles of gin and whisky very effectively.

Equity diary – You've paid for it, so you might as well use the bloody thing, dear.

Pills – It is to be expected that at some point on tour an actor will get ill. And if one actor gets ill, all of them will. So it is very wise to have a hearty and healthy supply of drugs on you at all times. I would suggest taking something for most eventualities – coughs, flu, vomiting, headaches, malaria, whooping cough, gonorrhoea and snake poisoning. However, it is always wise to keep your medical supply a secret otherwise you will quickly turn into the company pharmacy, or even worse, the company pusher.

....

Actors – going through your lines on a bus does not count as a national tour.

....

Embracing Different Stages

Touring can be very disorientating. Not only will you be staying in many different hotels and digs, but you will also be performing in many different venues. This can be at once a wonderful experience, but also a wholly dizzying one. The best way to combat this is by embracing each stage as though it is a new lover. Just like exploring a new body, a new space has weaknesses, beauty spots, and most importantly, G-spots.

Every stage has a G-spot. This is the erogenous zone of the stage; an area which can be at once highly sensitive yet hugely powerful. When you know what a stage's G-spot feels like, you will be able to locate it quickly, and instantly use it to your advantage. Some practitioners don't even acknowledge that it exists, that they have no scientific proof that it aids a performance. But over the years I have seen the effect of this spot on actors and audiences – and have been blown away by its tremendous power.

The way to find a stage's G-spot is firstly to enter the auditorium and view the stage from every level and angle. The point of this is to find the place on stage where you will always be visible. This area will be a few feet wide and somewhere near the centre – but, depending on the specific shape of the stage, it is always in a slightly different location.

Once you have identified this location you should head on stage and stand in it. Then look out into the auditorium and imagine it is full of people. As you do this, breathe deeply and begin chanting some of your lines. Do a little bit of walking around in this area and continue chanting. At some point you will experience an exhilarating sensation – a sensation where you feel a release, where your whole voice sounds freer and more powerful than it ever has before. When you find this place you should carry on speaking and breathing, repeating your lines until you can no more. You may feel like you are going to lose control at any moment. This is perfectly natural – it is the natural state of drama taking over your body. As you keep repeating your lines you will eventually feel so overwhelmed with a sensation of euphoria that you will know you have found the stage's G-spot.

That night during your performance you should try and touch the G-spot as often as possible. It will make you feel alive, and you will reach a whole new level of performance. However, you must be careful not to spend too much time on it – as this can cause the inexperienced actor to lose control, and end up in a gibbering heap. Like any truly great technique, you have to know when to stop. Ideally, you should start gently by teasing it, and then slowly increase your time and dedication on it. And before long you will become a master at finding the theatrical G-spot.

Stages also have different-sized wing-spaces, and at each venue there will be changes to how backstage props and costumes are set out. It is always advisable to explore these areas before doing the show – and make sure you know where your quick-change costumes and props are laid out.

Actors – remember: what happens on tour goes on Twitter.

Friends of the Theatre

When touring you will often be invited for a free drink on the first night in each venue. These evenings will be attended by the 'friends of the theatre' – who are a group of old dears who like to touch and dribble all over the actors. Of course, some actors thrive on such activity, getting deep thrills from the joyful enthusiasm of the local burghers, but other actors hide in the theatre toilets, praying never to be cuddled by the local bearded lady. You should always remember that there is nothing wrong with the local bearded lady. She is usually a very well-respected member of the community – and is often the mayor. And you don't want to ignore the mayor – beard or no beard, dear – as hanging out with them will get you in the local paper.

During these free drinks there will be a speech by the president of the 'friends of the theatre', complimenting the actors on their show. This speech tends to go on for quite a while, and is rather reminiscent of a school assembly – unless, of course, the show is not deemed 'good' in the eyes of the friends. In which case there won't be a speech. Or any free nuts, dear.

....

Actors – when touring you are a source of fascination for the locals. If they ask to touch you, please comply.

....

Pub Etiquette

One of the most important pastimes in an actor's life is the time spent in public houses. Whether it be on tour, during rehearsals, or simply between jobs, a good pub or bar can become a place of sanctity and contemplation. It is also a marvellous place to meet with other actors and discuss scurrilous gossip and upcoming castings. And, of course, to find out who is sleeping with who.

I remember the days of marvellous theatrical hellraisers – actors like Richard Harris, Oliver Reed, Peter O'Toole and Richard Burton. They were proper thespian boozers who would often stagger on and off stage or set. Although I would be whipped if I made any suggestion that drinking whilst working is acceptable, their binges and stories are the things of legend – and there was always gossip and speculation about them. These days actors much prefer to detox, go on yoga retreats and suck on celery sticks. Whilst this is healthier it certainly isn't as entertaining.

It is essential that anyone involved in theatre possesses good pub etiquette. An ignorance in this important practice results in isolation, bullying and a severe lack of respect from the rest of the company. Just as it is vital you 'play the game' in rehearsals, it is essential you do the same in the pub.

The Round Rule

Many actors, particularly those just graduating from drama school, will not fully appreciate the importance of the honourable and sacred tradition of the round rule. When in a drinking establishment, people take it in turns to buy everyone else at the table a drink. Sometimes you may think this rule a little peculiar – especially when buying for a large number of people – but it always tends to even itself out. A simple way of gaining admiration from the rest of the company is by being the first person to buy a round. It is particularly essential to be proactive in your 'buying' regime when the director is present. Many directors employ actors solely on their round-buying expertise.

Whilst new graduates may feel that they are spending an awful amount of money on their drinking habits, the sooner they realise the importance of this pastime, the better.

It is very easy for an actor to get a reputation for being 'tight' and 'stingy'. You can always spot a potentially tight actor as they will be the last ones to arrive at the bar (after everyone else has bought the drinks). They also disappear to the toilet for ten minutes if it's their round, and will have lots of convenient phone calls during the evening. They will go to monumental lengths to avoid spending money on anyone other than themselves. You should always make sure you are not marked with the 'stingy' title.

It is always advisable to go to the pub a few times early on in the rehearsal period. This is the time when 'company bonding' begins, and it is the perfect opportunity to flirt. Often my casting director likes to accompany the actors on their first pub visit – and accepts drinks from everyone. This can be very telling, and I know for a fact that the actor who flirts most with my casting director will be called in to audition for the next few shows.

A word of warning: Never sing or go through your lines loudly in the pub – as this causes members of the public to leave and the landlord to get angry. A pub is not the set of *Fame*. Flamboyant dancing and singing is not acceptable. It is even illegal in some countries and can result in the messy removal of jazz hands, dear.

Actors – don't drink and drama, dear.

When the Job Ends

After being in a job for a few months, your company becomes like a little family. And in this family you feel safe. And important. Every night you have a place to go: a place to perform and work – with people that you like and trust. After this has been going on for months it becomes a pattern, a habit – and when this is suddenly taken away from you it is a shock to the system.

My good friend Doctor Theatre always tells me that actors and people working on a show usually get ill the week after the show finishes. It is like your body knows when it has ended. Then, of course, you find yourself in that depressing position of being at home, unemployed and feeling ill.

This is where the concept of 'resting' comes from. The term 'resting' infuriates actors as it implies that when they are not acting they just lounge about at home in their smoking jackets, sipping whisky and nibbling on exotic fruits that are being fed to them by dwarfs. Sadly, this is not true – unless you are Kevin Spacey, in which case it is a weekly ritual. But for most actors the opposite is true. When an actor knows a show is coming to an end they have to find another way of getting an income, so they will telephone bars, promotional agencies, telemarketing companies, restaurants, front-of-house managers, temp agencies, escort agencies, the Houses of Parliament – anything that will help them pay the rent.

Of course, there are some lucky actors who are fortunate enough never to have to do this. They simply move from one acting job to the next. These kinds of actors invariably have a TV career, are represented by one of the top agents, and are known in the business as 'jammy gits'.

When a fellow actor says, 'Let's stay in touch, it's been such a pleasure,' chances are you won't, and it wasn't, dear.

ACT FOUR: IMPORTANT PEOPLE AND HOW TO DEAL WITH THEM

OR
PANTING, PLEADING, PRAYING, PRETENDING, PONTIFICATING, PURSUING AND PUSHING

It's lonely at the top. But you eat better, dear.

Agents

Many actors believe that agents are the key to a good career. Certainly having a good one will help – but if you can't read, write, and have no real talent, then an agent won't help at all. Unless you are Jordan. But she's not an actress. She's a joke, dear.

Agents on the whole are very nice people. Most of them will have been in the business for a number of years – many being old performers themselves. Having an agent who used to be an actor is useful in some ways, and awful in others. They will understand the frustrations of working for Equity minimum, but will also have moments of deep jealousy about your guest role in *Doctors*. Indeed, I have heard numerous stories about agents who have got so jealous of their clients that they've started representing themselves. This can be very awkward, particularly when you go in for a casting only to realise that your agent is up for the same role as you.

Agents come in all shapes and sizes. There are square ones, circular ones and triangular-shaped ones. I always think it is useful for potential clients to know what an agent looks like, which is why I'm trying to convince Spotlight to have a new agents division. *Spotlight for Agents* will be a book and website that contains every agents' headshot and CV – so actors can see where their potential agent trained, where their office is, and where they lost their virginity. This is hugely important – as you don't want to be represented by someone who lost their virginity in Morrisons.

An actor is only as good as their agent. And an agent is only as good as their actors.

As a general rule, the best agents have the strangest names. There are agencies called Troika, United, CAM, Markham, Frogatt & Irwin (MFI), Sainou, Gordon & French, Lou Coulson, Conway van Gelder Grant, Curtis Brown, Holland & Barrett – the list goes on. Most of these names will have been decided on a pub crawl. Apparently a weird name is a mark of success. Which explains the popularity of Benedict Cumberbatch.

In truth, the best way of discovering what an agent is actually like is by looking for anagrams. I think the following is rather telling:

Amanda Howard Associates – Woo! Satanic drama ass-head
ARG – RAG
Bloomfields – Bold of slime
Cole Kitchenn – Leech Nick Not
Conway van Gelder Grant – Endanger cow vagrantly
Curtis Brown – Burnt cow sir
Diamond Management – To demeaning madman
Hamilton Hoddel – Hello odd hit man
Hatton McEwan – O neat watchman
Ken McReddie – End mere dick
Lowy Hamilton Artists – Tally-ho! I'm worst saint
Narrow Road – RADA or worn
Sainou – A I Nu So (say it fast and it's 'Anusol')
Troika – Oar Kit
United – Nude It / Untied
The William Morris Agency – Worthy, smellier magician

> Actors – when in bed with an agent it is vital you call them by their correct name. A Troika does not like to be called a Curtis Brown, dear.

It is also advisable to do your background checks on agents. Check their website and see which actors they represent. Find out where they live and what they did before becoming an agent. It is no good being represented by an agent who used to be a greengrocer. Unless they used to supply fruit to all the best casting directors, in which case they would be a marvellous choice. When going to meet a potential agent always make sure you don't appear drunk. Agents, on the whole, admire actors who can at least appear sober.

Always remember: your agent works for *you*. Many actors forget this, and live in permanent fear of them. This is not healthy. The agent and the actor should have an equal relationship. It is like a healthy marriage, where the agent supports, nurtures and loves their actor. Of course, in marriage, sex is a big factor – and usually this is not part of the deal when signing with an agent. However, some agents, particularly in the Soho and Fitzrovia areas of London, like indulging in naughty activities with their clients.

The agent is there to represent *you*, and help carve *your* career. If you are with an agent who forces you to go to every single audition and accept every job, then they are not thinking about your long-term career. In fact, they are just thinking about the quickest way to get money to pay for their new wooden floor.

Most agents will be members of the PMA – which stands for the Personal Managers' Association. This is a very important body that serves to make agents practise fairly and honestly. I know one agent who calls them the 'Pretentious Managers' Adulterous Society' – although I have no idea where the extra 'S' came from. Many agents now also look after 'creatives'.

The word 'creatives' covers a multitude of people from directors, writers, choreographers, casting directors and young gay men.

Usually, agents will want to see you perform before offering representation. It is rare for an agent to represent you without seeing you in anything. Unless you are incredibly beautiful. Or their child. Over the years I have heard many actors complain about the catch-22 situation – where they can't get a job because they haven't got an agent, and can't get an agent because they haven't got a job. This is very tricky and requires a plan of action. One of the best things to do is to get a decent part in a fringe production – something that shows you off well – and invite an agent along to see you. However, if you feel you can't afford to work for nothing, simply get a job in The Groucho, The Ivy, Soho House or Century – and you are bound to serve an agent. Get speaking to them, give them free shots, laugh at their jokes, and utilise the skill of 'bottom licking'. If you are successful you will get a phone call the following day. If you are not, just repeat the exercise until they give in.

Once you have secured an agent it is wise to study the art of 'keeping an agent'. Agents are a difficult species, and whilst they are there to work for you, you are also there to earn money for them. The truth is that whilst you may be talented and have a good look, there are another ten people out there who are just as talented and good looking. So make sure they don't feel the need to fill your slot in. One way of doing this is by buying them nice presents – nothing too expensive, but they tend to like red wine, chocolates and season tickets to the opera.

Agents, in their defence, do have a difficult job. As well as trying to find work for their clients, they have to get on with every casting director, producer and creative out there – as potentially all of them could be offering their actors work.

They also have to be multiskilled. As well as reading and writing it is essential they are proficient at remembering things. Most agents will represent a large number of clients –

and with that comes the responsibility of remembering them all. That is harder than it sounds. Agents who have a particularly weak memory solve this problem by pinning their actors' headshots and names on a wall in their office. This avoids embarrassment. However, this is only a solution when in the office. It is a whole different ball game when wandering out and about in the big wide world. There is nothing more embarrassing than an agent introducing themselves to an actor after a show only to realise they represent that person already. It happens frequently, and usually results in a fist-fight outside the The Nell pub after closing time.

It is important to know that most agents will take commission for work whether they found it for you or not. This means that if you somehow manage to secure a marvellous advert or play by yourself, your agent will still take commission. Whilst this seems unfair, their argument is that they are always working for you, submitting you for things, and have the arduous task of remembering your name.

The usual commission rates for agents in London today are:

Theatre – 10%
Commercial theatre/voice-over/corporate – 12.5%
Percentage of your wife or husband's salary – 13%
TV, film, commericals – 15%
Any winnings on the lottery (or other forms of gambling) – 15%

Your agent is also legally allowed to help themselves to three items of furniture from your house every year, two DVDs whenever they want, the loan of your car when required, and an evening of passionate bedroom activity with your partner twice a month. Of course, this is just what the top London agents insist on; some of the smaller ones will make do with a little grope once a month, dear.

Agents also take commission on holiday pay – which is paid at the end of a contract. And why do they take commission on this? So they can afford a nicer hotel on their holiday in the Maldives.

A new popular trend in London is the Agent Swinger Evening. This is where agents take their most prized actors to a secret location – and swap them. I haven't been to one yet, but have heard countless rumours about these naughty evenings. The kinky thing about them is that the actors wear face masks – and nothing else. Throughout the evening, actors perform sonnets, sing, dance, and simply jump up and down. It's a little like *The Voice* – with the added joy of being able to view the actor's naughty bits. This is just another way of actors finding work and getting a better agent – and since competition is so high, the waiting list for these evenings is huge. Of course, casting directors are also invited, but I'm told that they just sit at the back dribbling.

Don't blame it on the sunshine, don't blame it on the moonlight, don't blame it on the good times. Blame it on your agent, dear.

The relationship between an agent and casting director is just like that of a boy and a girl, or a boy and a boy, or a girl and a girl – it is an old-fashioned mating ritual. Agents have to flatter the casting director, flirt with them, take them out on dates, get to know them, and offer them some sort of physical affection (ranging from gentle petting to something far more intimate). And this does not just happen overnight.

The agent will usually make the first move. If an agent has a client they think is right for a specific role, or they just want their client to have a 'general' meeting with a casting director, they will firstly send an email to the casting director. This may result in two things – either the casting director will give in to the agent's advances and agree to meet with their client, or they will play hard to get and ignore them. This can be quite difficult for the agent, especially if they hear that a better-looking agent has been more successful. But a good agent, just like a good lover, will never give up.

A dedicated agent will then try his charm by taking the casting director out on a date. The date will involve a little drink, possibly a meal (if the agent is really trying to impress), followed by a show. The agent will obviously be the one who pays for everything as he or she is the one trying to impress. The casting director, in honesty, is just there for the free meal.

If the evening proves successful, the agent will push the relationship to the next level – and introduce a third person. This person will be a client of theirs, who just happens to be in the show that the agent and casting director have watched. This is the perfect time for the agent to sell their client and allow the casting director to see why they should be excited by this new person. Most casting directors love a good threesome after a few glasses of Chardonnay, dear.

This mating ritual takes a lot of time and dedication to perfect – just as you would expect from any love affair – and new agents have to work on their mating technique. When an agent starts out, they are the new kid on the block and have to find new friends and enemies. It always takes a little while for them to be known and trusted by casting directors and directors. A casting director always takes a gamble when they get new actors and actresses in to audition, and because there are so many out there it is understandable why they tend to 'stick to what they know'. There is also a tendency for them to give new actors straight out of drama school a chance at leading roles – rather than a seasoned actor who only has supporting roles on their CV. I have spoken to various casting directors who admit they are more likely to audition actors who have just graduated from drama school – or who are new on the acting scene – than an actor with five years' worth of theatre credits on his CV. And this is the problem – an actor gets typecast straight away.

Some people argue that it is better to be working than doing some form of temp work, but some of the bigger agents will not allow their clients to take small-scale theatre work. Indeed, these agents make it clear in the first interview with actors that they will only allow them to do film or TV work – and whilst this must be frustrating for the new actor, you can also understand this tactic. I suppose the thing to consider is this – would you be happier working in theatre for two years, or doing a few weeks of TV work? It also depends on what kind of credits you are looking to put on your CV. In my opinion, work leads to work. So go out there, make the contacts, and do what you trained to do, dear.

It struck me recently, when browsing through some theatre programmes, that actors are often listed as 'cast' and the directors, choreographers, assistant directors, marketing managers, lighting designers and cleaning company are all listed as 'creatives'. It implies that being an actor is not creative. Although I am sometimes rather harsh on actors, they are the people that do the creating in rehearsals and create their performances. Theatre is a team effort – and without the combined skill and resources of everyone involved, the production would not happen. So, in future, I will get rid of the 'creative' and 'cast' divide – and call everyone a creative, dear!

Actors – the director is always on your side.
unless you are doing a bad job. Then they hate you, dear.

Directors

It is as tricky to become a director as it is to become an actor. There are many types of directors, and each one has their own responsibilities and resources. Of course some of them are not actually directors but glorified tea-makers, because, as in any profession, directors have to start from the bottom and work their way up. Though, in truth, I wish some of them had just continued making the tea.

Different Types of Directors

The **director** is the person whose name is on the posters and programmes. They are the ones who help sell the show and hopefully come with a great deal of experience. To be a director it is expected that you have gone to Cambridge or Oxford, and are capable of using long words on a daily basis. It helps if you wear glasses and own a plethora of scarves. It is also useful if you have interesting ideas for a play – although this is not essential as you will have an assistant stage manager to help if you get stuck. Most directors will have done some work assisting other directors at the RSC and RAC. The director is allowed to have good ideas, but must never be more creative than the producer.

The **assistant director** is employed to sit far away from the director and make notes on what is happening in the rehearsal room. Sometimes they will be given menial tasks like buying biscuits, cleaning actors, or reading aloud from the script when someone is ill. On special occasions they may even be allowed to offer advice and thoughts on a scene. I must admit an assistant director has a very difficult job. They have to be highly diplomatic, and even if they feel that the director's decision to base *Macbeth* in a fast-food chain is ridiculous, they must support that vision. However, assistant directors often come into their own on afternoons when the director falls asleep – which is why there is such a long queue to assist Sir Peter Hall, dear.

The **resident director** has the unenviable task of keeping check on a show and maintaining it to the quality of when it opened. Which can be very easy if the show was rubbish. But the resident director cannot re-direct anything – they have to stick with whatever has gone before them. It is their job to watch over a show and make sure that the actors are not being naughty. Their role is particularly important on a tour and in a long-running show, as this is when actors have the tendency to get bored and change things. Also the resident director will feel obliged to keep the company's 'spirits up'.

Resident directors are usually actors who want a bit of respect, and they think that becoming a resident director will give them that. It won't. Particularly if they are a gibbering fool who wants to be everybody's friend. That is not the role of the resident director. Their role is simple: keep the show in check. Nothing more, nothing less. However, I have known some resident directors who approach the rehearsals with a unique energy and freshness, actively encouraging the actors to keep their performances individual and new. Sadly these types of resident directors get sacked rather quickly to prevent the proper director feeling threatened.

Sometimes an **associate director** is employed to add their own 'take' on the show, and perhaps aid and assist the director. They are not quite fully fledged directors and are usually only employed on big shows, particularly when there is a cast change. In successful West End musicals and plays that last for a few years, the show is obviously recast a few times. This is done for two reasons: firstly, if the original cast stay in a show it can become stale and tired, and secondly, my casting director gets bored of staring at the same young boys year after year, so needs new eye candy.

It is usual in these kinds of shows that some of the cast stay and some leave. Sometimes this will be done of their own choosing, and sometimes they will not be asked to renew their contracts. It all depends on how well behaved they have been throughout the year, and how many times they have been nice to my mum.

An associate director is particularly useful during these cast changes. They will have been involved with the show from the start, so will know exactly how it is meant to look. It is always very difficult getting the original director back as they will be busy on other projects – so the associate takes over. However, sometimes the original director will grace the company with their presence for a day of rehearsals to give general notes – purely so they feel the show is still their own. Some directors only work on the big shows because they are potentially big money-making opportunities. As do the producers. Well, I have to pay for my Dom supply somehow, dear.

So, the associate director will spend their time playing, moving, and fiddling with the actors. But, of course, they will not be doing this job on their own – they will have the support of the assistant director. And the musical director. And the assistant musical director. And the associate musical director. And the choreographer. And the assistant choreographer. And the dance captain. And the company manager. And the ASM. In fact, there are sometimes more people directing the show than there are *in* the show, dear. But always remember to take the notes from the person whose opinions really matter, the person who pays your wages: the producer.

I must admit that I often wish I was a director. I love nothing more than strolling into the rehearsal room and seeing eager, excitable actors gazing at me for approval. I always smile back and offer wise words of encouragement, unless I don't like them. It is always very useful for me to sit in the rehearsal room – as it allows me to see if the director is doing what I've told them to do. In most cases the director will have told me their thoughts on the show, and only when I'm happy will they be allowed to proceed. If I ever go into a rehearsal room and see that they are being too inventive, I have to remind them of their role. I don't pay the directors to create *their* show. I pay them to create *my* show.

Nowadays it is true that it is just as important to have a well-known director as it is to have successful actors. I employ directors because it's trendy to have their names on the posters – even if they're not actually very good at directing. The public love seeing a show that has been directed by a film director, as that implies that they must be very good indeed. Although, in truth, they are often not. They just happen to be sharing a bed with someone who is, dear.

Actors – you know you've made it when the
musical director changes the key for you, dear.

Musical Directors

Musical directors are a unique breed of human life form.
They are inevitably very gifted musically, as a result of
spending years in solitude playing with their instrument. In
fact, some of them are so talented they will have spent years
playing with two of their instruments. Sometimes even at
the same time. And that's why they demand the big bucks.
And believe me – they demand the big bucks, dear.

Musicians and musical directors are very lucky in that they
have a superior being looking after them at all times. They
have a higher god, a defender, a department of the justice
system that they can always rely on. And because of this they
can demand marvellous pay packets for playing only four
notes in the overture of *Oklahoma!* Of course, I am referring
to the Musicians' Union.

The MU is a solid union. It has strict policies and guidelines
about when and where their members can work – and for
how long they can rehearse before breaking or going into
overtime. And because musicians know they are represented
by such an effective body, they will simply down instruments
and walk out when rehearsals run over. I recently witnessed
a tuba player dropping his instrument halfway through a
blow – which left a very disappointed actor standing with
his pants down.

Musicians are a skilled bunch and without them a musical,
or indeed any show using music, simply wouldn't work.
There is nothing as thrilling as hearing the triumphant
blasts of an overture as it builds the anticipation before a
show. I love it. The truth is that most of the shows in the
West End, and indeed touring at present, are musicals – and
without the dedication and talent of musicians and musical
directors they simply wouldn't be possible.

Although most musical directors are skilled musicians, it does not mean that they are all talented. In fact, I knew one musical director who couldn't even play an instrument – he just used the pre-recorded demos on his PSR400 Yamaha keyboard to take warm-ups, and got his mum to record all the music from the show the night before. No one dared question him – as no one questions the musical director, dear.

Different Types of Musical Directors

A good **musical director** will have passed their Grade 5 theory and piano exams. They will be able to read music, and be able to speak about different time signatures. They won't necessarily know what key they are playing in, but will know whether they are playing in major or minor. They will also understand that talking about the black notes on a piano is not racist. The main job of the musical director is to employ the best musicians who can play the score – and if this is done correctly it makes their life very easy indeed. It is essential they own a nice suit and tuxedo, and can waft their arms around in a convincing way. It is not, however, vital that they have an affair with Katherine Jenkins – although this is rather good for publicity.

A good **assistant musical director** will be able to play 'Chopsticks' on the piano, and be able to identify all the different sections of an orchestra. They will also be familiar with every musical scale and know how to use the 'transpose' function on a keyboard. It is a huge advantage if they can play the scale of C major but, of course, are not expected to know C minor – as that is what the musical supervisor is for.

A **musical supervisor** will be in charge of the overall 'sound' and 'feel' of a show. They will be highly experienced in all aspects of music – and will know the difference between baroque and pop music simply by listening to it. As a general rule, they will have passed both their GCSE and A-level Music exams, and will have followed this by attending a music conservatoire where they will have spent several years smoking lots of naughty substances and perfecting their fingering skills.

Many musical supervisors will help with the arrangements of the music, and often listen in during rehearsals to make sure the songs are 'balanced' correctly. By this I mean that the number of tenors, baritones, altos and sopranos are correct. There are many musical supervisors who claim to have perfect pitch, and will sit in rehearsals telling people that they are slightly flat or sharp. I remember one particularly embarrassing occasion when my musical supervisor stopped a song and accused an actress of being 'very flat'. My casting director, thinking the musical supervisor had said 'very fat', tried to defend the actress by saying, 'She's not very fat. She's just a bit chubby.' Awkward, dear.

Another type of musical director is the **children's musical director**. This person is employed solely to look after the children of the company, and also those older actors who behave like children (of whom there are an alarmingly large number). The children's musical director will be aged ten and over and will be highly skilled at playing the descant recorder. They will also be the person that sings the upper harmony line whenever 'Happy Birthday' is sung – which is essential when attending all the children's parties. It is a bonus if they can make balloon animals.

Finally, one of the main responsibilities of all types of musical director is to teach people the difference between an actor and a musician. Which is at least £300 a week.

....

Actors – 'I can't, I'm rehearsing' is not a valid excuse for missing the birth of your child. Unless you're rehearsing for the National, of course, dear.

....

Casting Directors

Casting directors are a new breed that was developed by Andrew Lloyd Webber a few years ago when he wanted an actor who could act, dance, sing, look good, roller skate and play the tuba. He didn't know any actors that specific so enlisted the help of a man he found hanging around some bins in Soho.

Casting directors have a very hard job. They have to look at headshots, watch plays and showreels, book audition rooms and speak to actors. That is not as easy as it sounds – as some actors are notoriously difficult to talk to, particularly those that have only done a one-year training course. In fact, even those that have done a three-year course sometimes find talking a challenge. But the actors that find talking the most difficult are international students – the ones that are only accepted into drama schools because they pay nearly double the fees of everyone else. When we audition these 'internationals' we ask them to audition in English, and not their native tongue. And if they can't do that we just ask them to jump up and down for a bit, dear.

Casting directors will usually have a pool of actors and agents they like to use. These agents are the ones they trust and, most importantly, give them the most expensive presents at Christmas. There are a handful of top agents that certain casting directors use, and only when these agents have been used are other ones approached. These kinds of agents represent a lot of celebrities – and this can be a very useful bargaining tool. If a casting director wants a certain celebrity, the good agent will insist on the casting director seeing another two of their clients. Marvellous if your agent represents Brad Pitt – but not so good if your agent represents Barry from *EastEnders*.

On very rare occasions your agent will surprise you and bring a casting director to your show. This is very useful as it allows you to meet and hopefully impress a casting director you haven't come across before. Sadly, the main casting directors will usually be too busy watching *Hollyoaks* to attend, so will send their assistant. And the assistant will only come along to get some free drinks. Invariably the assistant is someone who has no interest in theatre and is solely employed to do admin in the office, so in terms of helping your career is actually pretty useless, unless you need some photocopying doing.

Actors should always be nice to casting directors, as they are some of the most important people in the business. In fact, it could be argued that they are the *most* important people. They decide who is going to be seen for an audition – and, more importantly, who is *not* going to be seen. Casting directors tend to have rather good memories, so if you keep doing bad auditions they will remember, and only call you in when they are trying to fill up the numbers.

Different Types of Casting Directors

The corpse sits behind their desk and stares blankly at you no matter what you are doing. They will not speak, and only smile if the director forces them too. They will occasionally look down at their laptop and give the appearance of making notes – but in actual fact are just searching the internet for porn.

The enthusiast is great fun. They are genuinely very excited to see everyone, and will always do their best to make everyone feel comfortable. If you say something funny, they will laugh like it's the funniest thing they have ever heard. And if you sing well they will give you a standing ovation. But be warned. If you are bad, they will mark you off in their little black book and they will never see you ever again.

The musical-theatre casting director is either a middle-aged gay man or an elegant older woman. They cast all the big musicals in town, and between them decide which actors will be appearing in the West End. They are hugely influential, and some of them also help in the production side of things – so are very important to please. Always be careful that you don't get on the bad side of any of them, as the word will quickly spread between them. Even though they all work for different producers, most of them are good friends. Some of them even go on holiday together and spend days relaxing by the pool in their respective musical-theatre thongs.

Actors – please remember: the director is always right, unless the producer says they're not, dear.

Producers

Producers are the nicest people in the business. They are honest businesspeople who are involved in entertainment because they love everything about it, and have a genuine desire to create wonderful work. And they are always extremely good looking. Oh sorry – that's just me!

Sadly, not all producers are lovely and beautiful, but most of them certainly share something in common: a huge passion for theatre. A theatre producer oversees all aspects of mounting a theatre production. They find the script and option the show from the playwright, oversee the casting process, select a director and creative team, and secure funds for the production. Sometimes, if a show is small, the financing can be done entirely by the main producer, but this is rare. We usually bring investors in to the production in a limited partnership agreement, who all help finance the show together.

Different Types of Producers

The **producer** has their name above the title of the show on posters. They are the main people who finance the production and have overseen most aspects of putting it on.

You can tell how successful a producer is by the type of coat they are wearing. A denim jacket from ASDA means they are new and young at producing, and tend to concentrate on new work. A luxurious mink coat means they are doing very well indeed and possibly own some theatres in the West End.

The **associate producer** will be involved in the production in a significant way – perhaps by finding the star, the venue for the show, or even discovering the show itself. They will again be involved in the whole process of creating the show, but will not be overseeing it like the lead producer. You can always spot the associate producer as they are the person frantically frowning and flapping their arms behind the main producer, who has a tendency to ignore them.

An **assistant producer** tends to be a lot younger, and do many jobs ranging from organising rehearsal spaces to clipping the main producer's toenails.

I am often asked, 'How do you decide on what show to produce? Is it the script, the music, the venue, or the stars?' Truthfully, it is all of those things – mixed with a strong feeling in my gut. If my gut tells me that a show has something special and will have mass appeal, I will be extremely interested. However, my 'gut' method becomes unreliable when I eat pasta as I get bloated. So I never make important decisions after lunch, dear.

One of the most important things I consider is subject matter; what the show is about. There is no point in me producing anything that would only interest twenty people and their dogs. The show has to have a theme and story that will move and touch a huge number of people. And crucially it has to interest them enough to make them buy a ticket. I have been involved in many shows that have gone through an initial development stage, had money pumped into them, only for them to be deemed 'not quite right' at the last minute. When this is the case it is far better to lose the few thousand already spent, than invest millions more into a show that will eventually never even cover costs.

The name of the show is also very important. As silly as it sounds, if a show doesn't have a catchy title then no one will go and watch it. That's why I avoid shows that have the words 'bottom', 'poo' and 'love never dies' in the title. Shows that have a well-known title, or are a stage version of a film or television series are already interesting to an audience as they are recognisable (as long as that show isn't *Eldorado* or *Crossroads*). By the same token, many of the new jukebox musicals do so well as they already have a tailor-made audience – and are guaranteed to sell lots of tickets to the pre-existing fan base.

Finances are obviously hugely important. As well as the start-up money – which can be anywhere from £350,000 to £500,000 for plays, and around £5 million plus for big musicals – you have to have money in reserve to keep the show going. To give you a rough idea, weekly running costs can be £150,000 upwards (more if it's a big musical), which includes approximately £35,000 for contractors. There is no guarantee that the show will sell out, or even cover running costs to begin with, so it is vital to have money in the bank to keep it running for a period of time. This is essential, as it allows word of mouth to spread, which eventually equates to ticket sales. There is a saying, 'The shorter the run, the higher the gamble', dear.

Of course, there are ways to make the money back – by touring shows after they have had a stint in the West End. Shows often sell much better on tour, and many shows that don't sell in London are big box-office hits out of town. This is largely because the West End and the touring circuit are aimed at two very different audiences. In London, you are aiming a show at tourists and theatre devotees, whilst on tour you are selling it to each community and catchment area. In reality, in a lot of these areas it is a lot cheaper for someone to visit their local theatre than paying for the expense of travelling to London, staying overnight and watching a show – so the lure of going to a local theatre is a lot stronger. I always feel enthusiastic about touring successful work from London to as many regional theatres as possible.

To be honest, it is new work that excites me the most. I adore the thrill of discovering and experiencing new shows – they are extremely important in keeping theatre current and moving it forward. But the main problem with new work is that it is new! And that is an extra challenge: selling new work to an audience who have no idea what the product actually is. When an audience go to see *We Will Rock You* they know they are going to be 'entertained' by Queen songs. If they've never heard of the songs before, or are not familiar with the composer, it takes a lot more convincing for them to purchase a ticket. Obviously, one way of dealing with this problem is by generating a lot of buzz.

Every successful show will have been marketed well. It is essential that a show looks and sounds attractive to the general public even before they know what it is about. This involves securing lots of press coverage, interviews for the actors on TV and radio, and huge amounts of promotional materials (flyers, posters, websites, women with the show's logo tattooed onto their bottoms). And, very importantly, the main image that is associated with the show has to be powerful and instantly recognisable. If any of the above isn't handled correctly, a show doesn't stand much chance of reaching its target audience – and consequently it won't sell. Which is not good for my Dom supply, dear.

There's going to be a new boy band soon made up entirely of voice teachers. One Diction.

ACT FIVE: THE BUSINESS

OR
TAUNTING, TEASING, TICKLING, TEMPING, TRYING, TAKING, TESTING AND TIRING

Actors – please remember: the tooth fairy is not an acting fairy. Leaving your headshot and CV under a pillow will not result in cash. Or an acting job, dear.

Headshots vs Headshits

According to a very dear actor friend, one of the most annoying things an agent can say is 'You need new headshots.' This is a standard phrase agents use when they've got nothing better to say – which is most of the time. It is never comforting to learn that your headshots are the one thing stopping you taking the theatrical world by storm. Most actors believe the reason they get a job is because of their talent, their work ethic, their professionalism, their CV, their voice – but many agents will convince you it's solely because of your headshot. This is pure fiction, although a good headshot will certainly help you get noticed.

Over the years I have seen thousands of headshots, particularly during castings. And I have come to the conclusion that there are actually two types: the Headshot and the Headshit. Headshots appear on Spotlight, your website, your agent's website, in theatre programmes, and in frames around your mother's house.

Walking into an audition looking nothing like your headshot is an absurd waste of everyone's time – and this is when your headshot becomes known as your head*shit*. It is no good having a photo that makes you look beautiful and interesting when in fact you are ugly and boring. Because eventually we will need someone who is ugly and boring! The purpose of a headshot is to sell *you*, so it has to be a true likeness.

There is no point having a headshot that was taken ten years ago – unless you are Arlene Phillips, as she doesn't age.

I recently heard a story about an actor who was invited to audition for the role of Oliver Twist because his headshot looked so perfect. But the actor who walked into the room was in his late fifties – the silly man hadn't changed his headshot since he was fourteen. However, in this instance, Rowan Atkinson was very lucky as they were still looking for a Fagin, dear.

A good headshot will be a close-up of your face that conveys your character and personality. Of course, you can have a selection of headshots – and this is useful, as it allows us to see all of your different looks. However, this does not mean you should have a headshot of you dressed as a woman, a man, an alien, a dog or Robert Downey Jnr. All the photos need to be of you, *as you*. I don't want a headshot of you blacked up from the recent revival of the *Black and White Minstrel Show*. For one thing it won't look like you. And for another thing, it's racist.

So, what do we look for in a good headshot? Firstly, it should be a nice open shot that shows your whole face. And secondly, it shouldn't make you look gormless. Unless you are gormless. In which case a gormless shot is perfect. Personally, I like headshots that are interesting and honest. My casting director likes headshots that are cute and boyish. But take no notice of him, dear.

If you are wondering how best to pose for your next headshot session, here is a practical guide to what you should be aiming for:

A straight acting headshot – Look serious. Have stubble. And floppy hair.

A musical-theatre headshot – Smile. Show your teeth. And cleavage (if you can fit it into shot).

A children's TV-presenter headshot – Do the biggest smile that is humanly possible. Show your teeth. Look quirky. And fondle a small child.

A film actor's headshot – Imagine you are smelling a fart. Pull your cheeks in. Pout. And look good.

If you are unhappy with your headshots you have two alternatives. Have new ones taken. Or have plastic surgery.

Some theatre companies have their own preferred type of headshot. For example, the National Theatre likes headshots displaying pitted skin and curly hair, the Donmar likes headshots that are cross-eyed and contain a monobrow, and all the male musical-theatre casting directors in the West End like headshots of pretty young men.

It's very naughty but my casting director will call people in just because of how good looking their headshot makes them. Whilst I don't completely agree with this, it does give us something to look forward to after lunch.

If your agent recommends a specific headshot photographer, they will undoubtedly have seen each other naked.

Some photographers charge ludicrous amounts of money – up to £1,000 in some cases. Is it worth it? Of course it isn't. Photographers are very clever, and will offer free sessions to celebrities so they can use their headshots in advertising. Just because a photographer has taken a photo of Noel Edmonds playing with Mr Blobby it doesn't mean they are any good. I never understand why poor actors want to spend hundreds of pounds on a set of new headshot photos when they can't even afford to eat at Pizza Express.

The only difference between expensive headshot photographers and cheaper ones is that the expensive ones have nicer houses. I understand that many people think a good photographer will have a nice studio, put you at ease, and catch you at your most natural. This is a very valid point. But I can make anyone feel relaxed by plying them with alcohol. Also, you can go to any public park to have an outdoor headshot – and use the public lavatories as the setting for indoor shots – both of which are free, and rather kinky.

In truth, for £400 you could buy yourself a good camera, find a discreet area of your bedroom and get your partner to take some photos. It may take a while for them to figure out how to turn the thing on, but once they have, they're sure to take at least a couple of useable shots.

Websites vs Webshites

It has recently become increasingly important for actors to have personal websites. Indeed, many agents now insist on it. Websites are marvellous tools in selling yourself, connecting with others and increasing the public awareness of you. And, just like a sexually transmitted disease round the cast of *Mamma Mia!*, they can spread like wildfire, dear.

Your website should be eye-catching, informative and show lots of different photos of you in and out of role. It should allow someone to get a true representation of you as a performer – and should work as a perfect marketing tool. Because the internet is now such a huge part of our everyday lives, the importance of your website is paramount. Obviously, it is not the end of the world if you don't have one – but I think in time they will become as essential as your Equity subscription.

A good website will show your CV, your voicereel and showreel, a gallery, headshots, a biog and your contact details. Of course, it is advisable not to have your own personal mobile number on display – unless you want to be plagued with calls by sweaty young fans and casting directors. It's best to have your agent's details on your website. This way your agent gets to deal with those nagging phone calls from your mother when you've forgotten your niece's birthday.

Make your website nice and easy to navigate around – there is nothing worse than spending half an hour *attempting* to find your CV or headshot. In the end we will simply give up. My casting director frequently spends time Googling actors he is auditioning – during their actual audition. It is a very naughty habit, but I must say some of the half-naked images we find on Facebook do make you more likely to get a recall.

One of the biggest mistakes I have seen on websites is when actors give their thoughts on acting and the reason why they created certain characters. This is a classic feature of a web*shite*, as no one apart from you cares about how you reached your final performance – usually it will have been based on what frock you were wearing anyway. Of course, Antony Sher has spent a lifetime writing and recording his various methods and artistic endeavours, but people have only put up with that because it keeps him quiet.

The idea of actors' websites came over from America, as did the colour headshot. American actors tend to be very good and proactive at selling themselves. In the UK, actors feel more intimidated about putting themselves out there for fear of looking desperate. Sadly there is a feeling that you shouldn't push yourself too much, but I am inclined to disagree. It just depends on *how* you intend to push yourself. There is no point sending death threats to casting directors and directors. Those should only be sent to other actors who are up for the same role as you, dear.

Twitter and YouTube

Both Twitter and YouTube have suddenly become an important part of an actor's life. They are great marketing tools, and can aid you in promoting yourself and the work you are in. There are even some producers and directors who will check your number of Twitter followers and YouTube channel subscribers – as it is a good indicator of how popular you are. Again, it comes down to the simple business of getting 'bums on seats'. If you are an actor with 10,000 Twitter followers, you are more likely to get the job than an actor with only 100. Who you are, and how many people know who you are, regrettably becomes more important by the year, dear.

If you can only attract half a dozen followers, it might be better to get out and leave Twitter to the experts...

Actors – please avoid watching your showreel more than five times a day. It can lead to 'showreel compulsive disorder', dear.

Showreels

A showreel is a short video that showcases an actor's screen work, and they are becoming more and more essential, particularly to get work in TV and film. They are usually no more than five minutes long, and are put together with the purpose of 'showing off' an actor, so that casting directors can see what actors look like on screen.

Many actors often find themselves in a problematic situation – where they have no TV experience, and in order to get the experience they need a showreel. This is obviously very difficult, but with video cameras being so cheap, and out-of-work *Holby* directors so desperate for work, there are many ways of making showreels by yourself.

Firstly, there are people that offer 'showreel making' services. If you search the internet you can find many professional directors who will direct and edit your scenes for you. This kind of service usually costs around £300–500 depending on how many scenes you want filmed. All you have to do is choose your scenes and fellow actors – and they will provide the camera equipment, film and edit the scenes together for you. In fact, they will do everything apart from learning the lines and acting the scenes, which sadly is still your responsibility, dear.

Another way of assembling scenes for a showreel is by acting in student films. I have spoken to many people who have been involved in these – and have heard of varying levels of success. Some actors say you can never be sure about the quality of the finished film. But then the same can be said if you play a guest role in *Midsomer Murders*. The good thing about student films is that plenty of them are made, and some agents will even put their clients up for them. Of course, they involve auditioning just like 'real' work, but can be a marvellous way of building up lots of decent screentime. However, you must always be sure to read the script fully before agreeing to do them. Student films tend to involve crying, nudity, and aimless wandering around parks and London suburbs. Fine if you like aimless wandering, but pretty boring if you don't.

If you are making your own showreel, please avoid using footage from a recent holiday in Greece. Unless, of course, you find a really impressive setting and feel compelled to pretend you are in *Gladiator*. In which case you should go for it and give your best 'Russell Crowe'. But for God's sake don't sing whilst being Russell Crowe. As this always ends in tears, dear.

When deciding which scenes to use, it is essential they show you playing lots of different characters. If in doubt, an easy way of accomplishing this is by attaching an accessory to your face. For example, have one character wearing glasses, a second one with a moustache, another with stubble, another cleanly shaved, and a final one from America (if you can't do the accent just wear a tight vest with the star-spangled banner on it).

Another clever trick is to get some of your actor friends to wear masks of celebrities – and do a scene with them. Or you could edit together some clips of yourself with some clips of famous actors so it looks like you are acting in the same scene. This method has been used by many actors, and indeed formed the basis of Hugh Grant's early film career.

It is very important that your showreel looks professional and is of a high quality. I have seen many showreels recently that look amateurish and home-made. This is particularly obvious when the actor's mum and dad are playing all the other characters. Of course, this is fine if your mum is Judi Dench, but not so compelling if your mum is Kerry Katona.

Also, you should avoid filming yourself on an iPhone. It is always obvious when someone has done this as it is apparent they are holding the phone with one hand and acting with the other. Obviously you can get someone else to record you, but always ensure they have a steady hand. There is nothing worse than shaky showreels. They look like *The Blair Witch Project*, and make me feel giddy. Which results in me vomiting all over your headshot. And that is not very pleasant for anyone. Particularly your face, dear.

A word of warning: As a safety precaution you should always double-check the edit of your showreel before allowing it to be viewed. It is so very quick and easy to put work out there – indeed, it takes only a few minutes to upload a showreel online. Whilst this is marvellously time-efficient, it can also be extremely dangerous. I remember one horrific story where an actor uploaded his showreel only to receive a panicked call from his agent four hours later telling him that he'd actually uploaded a video of himself doing naughty things with his partner. Whilst this was hugely embarrassing for the actor in question, it did get him a sudden influx of auditions – and Russell Grant hasn't stopped working since.

There is a habit in showreels to feature funky music at the beginning with a montage of the actor in various roles. Be aware that this montage is viewed as a joke – as casting directors don't really want to watch actors gurning and flapping their arms around to random bits of pop music. I have heard of many careers being stopped short as a result of these first flimsy thirty seconds. It really is rather sad. Often showreel montages feature ridiculous close-ups of actors staring at the camera with varying degrees of intensity before hitting something and frantically running around in a jubilant manner. If we wanted to see that we would just find some footage of you getting drunk on YouTube. There is a saying in the business: 'A montage never displays good acting. A montage displays actors who think they are good at acting.' I don't know who said that, and I don't really know what it means, but it sounds rather impressive, dear.

In truth, the main use of a showreel is simply to show how you look on screen. It is surprising how different some actors actually appear on TV and film – which is why a showreel is vital in allowing the casting director and director to see what you look like. You'd never believe it, but in real life David Tennant is actually four-foot-two and black. The camera never lies – it just distorts reality, dear.

Finally, never have clips of you performing on *stage* on your showreel. Whilst this can be tempting, particularly if you are playing a leading role, it can have appalling results on the viewer. I have known casting directors spontaneously combust after seeing such footage. There is a major difference between stage acting and screen acting – and you don't want a beautifully subtle TV scene undermined by a ridiculously over-the-top scene from your last pantomime. Unless, of course, your screen scene is from *Doctors*, in which case a stage scene will be far subtler.

What's the difference between acting on stage and acting on film? At least £5,000, dear.

Acting for Camera

Acting for camera is a very different discipline to acting on stage. For one thing, if you are doing a film you get a Winnebago, a driver, more money, and intense jealousy from fellow performers.

There have been many guides over the years about the best techniques and methods for screen acting. It is common knowledge that you should not blink on screen, you should not look directly at the camera, you should never flap your arms too wildly, you should avoid smoking a cigarette (as it's a bugger for continuity), and you should speak as quietly as possible. Obviously, this advice is all the stuff of legend – and the only true way of learning screen acting is to do it *yourself*.

It is generally accepted that you should try and be smaller when acting on screen, and avoid those moments of huge gurning that work so wonderfully on stage. That is not to say that the odd gurn can't make an appearance – you just have to be very selective about when and where it is released. This is also the same for eyebrows. Eyebrows are the one body part that have a mind of their own on screen. You may think you have control of your facial features, but as soon as you find yourself in front of a camera your face will adopt a performance and physicality all of its own. This is something you will only realise when you watch footage of yourself.

Many actors spend years attempting to control their face – as they want to have that perfect 'still' look on camera. As an example, just watch the most celebrated film stars and their 'controlled' faces. Their eyebrows will only move on certain occasions, their eyes will only blink when they look down, and their nose will only flare when they are showing intense aggression. These kinds of sophisticated techniques are not learnt overnight, dear.

One of the best ways to control your face is by sitting in front of a mirror and staring at yourself. It is advisable to keep your clothes on for this practice – to prevent any unnecessary distraction. Once you feel comfortable, vocalise some lines and observe what happens to your face. The first thing you will notice is your face's athleticism – and whilst this is something to be applauded in children's theatre, it is not useful when filming *Silent Witness*.

You also have to be aware of the good and bad side of your face. Everybody has one of each, and those that say otherwise have two bad ones. Your good side should obviously be the side that sees more of the camera, and your bad side should be kept for more shocking, heartfelt and tense moments.

For every actor that wins an Oscar there are
another ten thousand living below the poverty line:
Equity minimum, dear.

Not blinking when acting on screen apparently makes you look more powerful. Personally, I think it makes you look like a robot. Next time you watch a film, observe the actors. You will notice their lack of blinking – particularly in close-ups. It is a very strange technique as actors always attempt to be 'real' – and in real life, people blink. So why shouldn't they blink on screen? I often worry for these 'non-blinking' actors – as they are preventing their eyelids from doing their natural function of cleaning and lubricating the eyes. Surely these non-blinking actors must spend their entire lives with eye infections? It explains why actors are so good at crying – it has nothing to do with emotional engagement with the character; it's just that they've all got hideous eye diseases caused from a lack of blinking.

Another technique for acting on screen is whispering. You will find that most screen actors whisper at such a low level that no one on set can actually hear what they are saying – apart from the sound guy. Whispering is a very useful tool as it means you don't actually move the rest of your face very much – giving you a look of subtle intensity. Consequently, there are now a lot of films where you can't actually hear what is being said. To be honest, this doesn't really bother me as I always take my iPod to the cinema so I can listen to *Les Mis* anyway. I also did this when I went to the *Les Mis* movie – so I could hear it in stereo.

Worryingly, those screen actors that mumble so inaudibly on screen have now started taking their talent onto our theatre stages. Which is why I always sit in the first five rows when I watch a play. Any further back and I can't understand a word of what is being said. In my opinion, if they can't be heard, stop paying them and get Donald Sinden in, dear.

Roses are red, violets are blue, I've been on TV, and I've done more than you.

Radio and Voice-over Work

There are many actors who, sadly, are not very nice to look at. They may attempt to use copious amounts of make-up and clever arrangements of their hair to hide this fact – but the truth is they will never play the romantic leads. This is why radio drama was invented – so ugly actors can play attractive parts. This is not to say that all voice-over actors are ugly. Of course they aren't. Some of them are beautiful. But they are just there to give the sound engineer something nice to stare at whilst fiddling with his knobs.

However, this does not mean that actors shouldn't attempt to look good for voice-over work. An actor must *always* try and look good, whether they are working in radio, television, theatre, or performing in a Goofy costume at Disneyland. They are actors – and it is an actor's duty to look good.

Radio and voice-over work is also a godsend for lazy actors – as lines don't need to be learned. In fact, I have often heard that the secret to great voice-over performances is to keep it sounding fresh and real. And for this reason many actors won't even bother reading the script before-hand, and will have no idea who their character is and what the play is about. Some call this being creative. I call it being bone idle.

Many actors are lucky enough to have a voice-over agent as well as their normal acting agent – which can lead to jealousy, envy and confusion. It is a very difficult thing to broach with your agent – particularly as many agencies now have both acting and voice-over departments. In fact, many agents now represent everything and everyone – actors, comedians, voice-over artists, writers, directors, children, dancers, presenters, plumbers, celebrities, cameramen, casting directors and designers. There are even agents who represent other agents, dear.

Before turning up for your recording session it is vital you have done sufficient preparation. Always make sure you can pronounce the words correctly – you don't want to turn up and say 'enema' wrong, particularly if the play is about colonic irrigation. I would suggest that you practise saying all difficult words out loud, so that your lips and tongue become accustomed to the feel of them.

There are different ways that radio plays are recorded – some of them are done in isolation booths, some in bigger studios, and some on location. Each has different vocal demands on the performer, but in every case your priority is to say the words clearly and in the correct order. Lots of times you will have the writer sitting in the studio watching you, and writers can get very tetchy when actors try to 'improve' the script.

In the final year of drama training, some lucky student actors are chosen to represent their school in the Carleton Hobbs Competition. This contest is run by BBC Radio – and the winner gets a place in their prestigious radio rep company. It is a marvellous opportunity for fresh new talent to gain valuable experience working for one of the best drama companies in the world. But, to be honest, even if you weren't in the Carleton Hobbs team you might as well say that you were – because everyone else does. It is one of the most common credits on an actor's CV, dear.

I have often been invited by eager friends to sit in studios and observe the whole voice-over process. And from these sessions I have seen first-hand the kind of mistakes that actors make.

One of the first things you have to be aware of is what you are wearing. There is no point wearing something that rattles or constantly rubs as you move – as this will be picked up by the mic. The microphones are so sensitive – particularly when recording in isolation booths – and because of this, you should also be careful not to snort, burp or fart.

Unless, of course, you don't like the person who is using the booth after you, dear.

Active hand gestures give the impression of professionalism. No one likes a voice-over artist who just stands there. Clever use of the hands makes everyone think you know exactly what you are doing. And is an excellent distraction from a bad accent. However, you must be careful not to move *too* much – as the microphones may pick it up. It's a very fine line. Excessive movement should only be used when your character is having an epileptic fit. This doesn't mean that you shouldn't be animated, but being animated and jumping up and down like a lunatic are two very different things.

Before your session, try and avoid eating dairy products as this will result in a 'phlegmy' performance. I heard about one instance where a spittoon had to be placed in front of an actor – as at the end of every line he had to get rid of excess mucus and lard. Not nice. Although they did make a nice profit by selling bottles of it on eBay to overenthusiastic Tom Baker fans.

The same attention should be paid to coffee. Coffee has a tendency to dry your mouth, which is not helpful when doing a radio recording. Of course, it can be marvellous if you are trying to sound like a water-starved character who has got lost in the desert, but in all other circumstances should be avoided.

You should never alter the script by adding your own dialogue. Whilst this may seem very tempting and make you feel more involved in the process, it puts you in a vulnerable position – because if the eventual recording is rubbish you will get the blame. It is vital that you *never* put yourself in a position where you can be blamed. Always make sure that someone else can be held responsible.

Avoid fiddling with the sound engineer and his buttons. Playing with either can result in permanent hand damage, dear.

Never attempt to move the microphone. This is what the sound engineer is for. And besides, the microphone is far too expensive for an actor to be playing around with. You will have no difficulty spotting the sound engineer. They will be the ones sitting behind the massive mixing desk twiddling with their knobs. As a general rule, they will be wearing an XXL T-shirt and always have a fascination with beautiful women. They are extremely nice people and have the ultimate control of your performance – so it is essential you are friendly to them. If, however, the sound engineer is rude to you, you should start miming halfway through your dialogue. This will cause huge panic, and everyone will think your microphone is broken. Great fun – especially after a long day, dear.

It is always advisable to have lots of interesting topics of conversation up your sleeve. When doing radio and television there will undoubtedly be long periods when you are sitting in a small room with lots of strangers – and this is the time when your social skills come to the fore. There is a general presumption that actors are marvellously confident and always have something interesting to say. This, sadly, is a little fib invented by Stanislavsky to make actors appear more interesting. I would suggest having a good read of a newspaper the day before, or at least scan the front page of *The Stage* so you've got a few topical things to talk about. Of course, it is marvellous if you know about – or can invent – a scandal, as this will make your gossip the main point of conversation throughout the day.

When recording, it is also advisable to let people know when you are planning a page turn. Turning a page can be a noisy affair, and if all the actors do it at the same time it produces a thunderous sound of paper shuffling, resulting in unnecessary retakes. If you stumble over some lines, just calmly go back to the beginning and start again. It really is not necessary to swear every time you go wrong, although if you do there is a chance you could end up in the outtakes. Outtakes themselves can be very lucrative – particularly in TV – with actors being paid as much as £500 each time a blooper clip is used. Some actors, of course, will use this money as an incentive to go wrong as often as possible. If you spot an actor going wrong for this reason they will usually have a rather large tax bill to pay.

I'm thinking of holding auditions in the West End after shows finish – at 10.30 p.m. Actors are already in London, and I'm sloshed by then. Perfect, dear.

Commercials

Auditioning for a commercial is unlike any other casting you will do, mainly because it is entirely about your look. The advert's only function is to sell the product – so if you look right, and convey the right image for a product, then you could potentially earn big money. Of course, just like there are many different types of actors, there are many different types of products. You could be one of the lucky ones who is perfect for an aftershave commercial, or you could be more unfortunate and find yourself as the face of the latest haemorrhoid cream, dear.

When auditioning for an advert you will be allotted a time like any other audition, but you should always be prepared to hang around for at least two hours. I have been reliably informed by almost every actor I know that commercial castings never run on time – in fact, it is against acting laws if they do. The castings themselves usually take place in dingy, mouldy rooms in Soho, and when you arrive you can be expected to be greeted by an unenthusiastic receptionist who finds any form of social communication difficult. This lovely person will hand you lots of pieces of paper to read and sign. These pieces of paper will be enquiring about what other commercials you have done recently, your age, name, agent's details, and phone number. Obviously it would be too much trouble for them to fill these forms in themselves

– as the people running the casting are too busy staring at YouTube. However, if you fill them in correctly you have passed the first test, and will be asked to stand and have a Polaroid of your face taken, so that the casting director and director can remind themselves of who you are.

When posing for this Polaroid it is advisable to look straight into the camera and not smile like a lunatic. If you do feel the need to smile, then make sure you haven't got any of your lunch lodged in your teeth. This can be particularly embarrassing, especially if you are at a casting for a dental hygiene advert.

Next comes the arduous task of sitting around and trying not to look bored for a few hours. This is the time when you can read the 'brief' or 'script'. The brief will comprise of a few lines about the product, followed by a page going into great detail about the advert, which has been done solely to convince you that it is a good idea. When you finally get into the audition room there will be a couple of casting assistants and the director. The casting assistants will introduce you to the director, who will usually be a cool-looking mid-thirty-year-old who is surrounded by empty Starbucks cups. Never come across as too enthusiastic at this stage, because they will never be enthusiastic to you. The director will look at you briefly, then ask you to stand in a spot in front of the camera. Everyone will smile politely at you for ten seconds until they get distracted by their coffee.

You will then be asked to do an 'ident', where you look into the camera and say your name, agent and sometimes age. You will also be asked to show your profiles, which means showing both sides of your face to the camera. Make sure you linger longer on your favourite side. If you do not have a favourite, just pick the one that is the least spotty.

Sometimes you may be asked to partner up with someone; they could be playing your lover and you instantly have to appear comfortable with them in any situation. This can be a problem if the person you are partnered with resembles an old scab. If this is the case, politely decline and ask the casting director if they can put you with someone better-looking. If this is not possible, you will have no choice but to rely on your acting skills.

You will frequently feel like you're making a fool of yourself in commercial castings, often for the amusement of the casting directors. But don't worry: most of them, in all honesty, barely take any notice anyway. The typical director of ads tends to be more concerned with the next movie or TV series they're working on – and only agree to do adverts for a bit of extra money. So in terms of passion and excitement, you'll be lucky if you get a smile from them, dear.

When your time arrives, and the camera is focused on you, waiting to see your best impression of a credit card, or your best premature ejaculation face, you simply have to think of the money. There are actors I know who have even changed their moral and ethical code because of good advert money. One actor got offered a McDonald's advert promoting a new burger, and because the money was so good he leapt at the chance. He spent the whole day biting into the most perfect-looking beefburger ever, and then smiled contentedly at the camera. After four hours of filming he got through forty burgers – which must be a world record for a strict vegetarian.

In terms of your performance, different rules apply in adverts. You will only know if you're being too big or too small when the director gives you feedback after your first take – but most adverts do not rely on delicate, subtle performances. Particularly if you are pretending to be a giant chicken breast. As a bit of general advice: be bold, be big, and don't take it too seriously.

After your casting I recommend having a stiff drink and forgetting about it. If you are lucky you may get a call the following day saying you have been 'pencilled'. A pencil means you are in the running for the advert, and you will be asked to keep the shooting dates free. However, a 'pencil' actually means nothing at all, as everyone gets them these days. Followed by a heavy pencil. Which again, means absolutely nothing. The terms 'pencil' and 'heavy pencil' were invented by casting directors as a way of keeping actors on hold until the director makes their mind up. Always remember: you haven't got the job until you've signed the contract, dear.

....

Actors – doing a workshop of a show doesn't mean you'll be in the final production. It just means you'll be in another workshop, dear.

....

Workshops

Many plays and musicals are now developed during workshops. Workshops are a period – lasting from a couple of days to several weeks – when a group of people come together to work on and develop a show. Usually the show will only have recently been written, and actors will be required to say lines out loud and sing songs *in tune* – so that the writer and director can hear what the piece sounds like 'off the page'.

These workshops are a way for directors and writers to play with actors for a few days whilst making them bring a new script to life. It is quite rare that workshops are actually paid – many are not and, like a lot of theatre these days, relies on the actors being prepared to share their talent for nothing. However, it's surprising how easy it is to bribe actors to do this. And the variety and quality of actors who often get involved is marvellous. I have supported many workshops – and am always thrilled with the high calibre of people who give up their time. This is possibly as they believe we will use them in the actual production. But, of course, we rarely do – because by then we'll be forced to replace them with someone off the telly.

When doing a workshop it is vital you are open and enthusiastic at all times. You will be told on day one that the writer and director welcome feedback – and that your input is essential in ensuring the show will 'work'. Of course, this is all rather lovely to hear, but in reality they only want to hear that you like their material. You should never make too many suggestions, and definitely never try and suggest changes to the plot or dialogue. Writers are very protective over their work, fearing any sort of criticism – particularly from the actors. It is far safer just to nod and congratulate them on the superb work they have created – and drop hints that you think they are the best playwright around. This increases your chance of appearing in the final show, and even them possibly writing you a part in their next project.

Recently it has become apparent that the trend in new musicals is to make them all very 'real' and 'gritty' – and they are either based on a farm or in an office. There tends to be at least one gay character, one person who is unsure about their sexuality, and one person who is contemplating suicide. But through the medium of close-harmony singing, everyone realises that life is not as bad as they thought, that people are entitled to be who they want to be, and that love is all around. And everyone lives happily ever after. How lovely, dear.

It is also common that young composers write the most complicated pieces of music possible – as though this is the secret to creating truly great songs. *It is not!* Marvellous show music does not have to be complicated musically – in fact, it is far more important that a musical has 'catchy' melodies. Just look at Andrew Lloyd Webber (if you can bear to). He knows exactly what he's doing. His chord progressions and structures are some of the most basic around – but they work triumphantly (with the exception of *Love Never Dies*, of course). And this is because he has blessed them all with tunes that stick. His melodies haunt, captivate, and stay with you for a lifetime. It doesn't have to be highbrow discordant chaos to have a lasting effect.

I am not insinuating that all songs written in a different key to C major are rubbish – of course not. Take Stephen Sondheim, for instance. A master of his craft. And his music is often very technically challenging. But, again, his melodies and music stay with you. The problem comes when you have some absurd nonsense that is filled with constant key and time-signature changes, confused melodies that can't make their mind up about what genre they are in, and chords that don't even make sense to Benjamin Britten. It really is a waste of time for everyone involved. In my mind, composers should keep it simple and effective – after all, the songs are meant to tell the story, not confuse it.

In workshops it is very rare that you perform the whole show. Usually you will stand and just perform excerpts, with the story, stage directions and character descriptions being read out by the director or writer. The aim is obviously to 'sell' the show to potential investors, so the best songs will have been chosen. If the best songs are actually bloody awful you should just smile politely and think of England.

After the performance it is theatrical law that wine and nibbles are served. This is when the wisest actors get their 'payment'. I suggest getting savagely sloshed by necking as much free wine as possible, stuffing whatever food and booze you can into your rucksack, and making a swift exit. I have known actors feeding themselves for years using this method, dear.

Never judge an actor on how much work they've done. Judge an actor on *what* work they've done, dear.

Biographies

There always comes a time in the rehearsal period when an actor will be asked to send their biography to the company manager, so they can be formatted and put into the programme. This task can be very difficult and time-consuming – especially if an actor decides to lie.

Actors never want to look like they are inexperienced, so the temptation to make credits up, or write ludicrous essays about their upbringing, seems like a clever idea. It isn't. In fact, lying on your biog is the worst thing you can do.

An actor's biography should simply list where you trained, followed by your professional credits, and nothing else. Basically we just want to see an appealing and concise version of your CV. It really isn't necessary to tell us how many GCSEs, A levels and degrees you have. Because in theatre these qualifications don't make a jot of difference, dear.

> It's not the length of your CV, it's what you do with it that counts, dear.

I have read many ridiculous biographies in my time. Of course, you can choose to write whatever you want – but you must always be aware that industry professionals, as well as your friends and family, will read it, so it is wise to make sure it doesn't sound too foolish. This is a lot easier than it sounds, particularly if you cannot read and write. If this is the case I suggest you use some crayons and make a nice drawing. It would be a welcome relief to have some lovely colourful drawings next to a headshot, and would certainly make me remember your name.

The most useful thing to remember when writing your biog is that a potential director or agent will read it, so only write what you think is appropriate. Avoid using swear words, racist insults and sexist remarks. Spelling mistakes are also very off-putting. I recently read a biog that said an actor had been in the original cast of *Chitty Chitty Gang Bang*. Lucky him, dear.

I am also not a fan of actors writing how 'thrilled' they are to be in a show, and how they'd like to thank their mummy and daddy, Grandma Winifred and Grandpa

Geoffrey for their constant support. The only person they should be thanking is the producer for giving them the job in the first place.

Actors who don't have many professional credits often make their biog longer by writing *every single character* they have ever played alongside the name of the production. It really looks very obvious, and isn't recommended – particularly if you are including characters such as 'Man Crossing Stage', 'Posh Lady Number 2' and 'Guy with Hat'.

Here is an example of a biog that breaks all the rules:

Candy Floss

Candy trained at RADA, LAMDA and Sylvia Young (foundation courses).

She has been involved in theatre since a young age, and was 'bitten by the bug' when she performed in her school production of *Bugsy Malone* at the age of five! Since applying that first bit of greasepaint she has never looked back! She quickly dedicated all of her spare time to learning all types of dance – and got a distinction in Major Preparatory Tap.

At the young age of seventeen Candy was chosen to do a schools' tour raising awareness of marine wildlife – entitled *Under the Seaweed* – where she spent six valuable months teaching kids what to do if they ever caught crabs. She loves nothing more than mixing her two passions – drama and small children.

Her work in entertainment has taken her worldwide, and she has been lucky enough to perform in such places as Hull, Minehead, Tenerife, Tehran and Brent Cross Shopping Centre.

Theatre includes: creating the role of Ophelia in *Hamlet* (RSC, Rochdale Shakespeare Company), Julie Andrews in *The Sound of Music* (Newcastle Operatic Society), Annie in *TrAnnie!* (Middle Eastern tour), u/s Vagina in *The Vagina Monologues* (primary schools' tour), *Pride and Prejudice* (Sylvia Young), Polly in *The Boy*

Friend (Sylvia Young), Mrs Macbeth in *Macbeth* (Westfield Shopping Centre).

Film: Fantine in *Les Misérables* (Universal Studios, Hull), Emma in *Emma* (BBC, Bradford Benevolent Collective), *Notting Will* (short), *Signed* (short), *Addition* (feature), *The World is Not Enough* (extra), *29 Days Later* (extra), *Gulliver's Travels* (extra), *Gladiator 2* (low-budget, short feature, extra).

TV: *The X Factor, Britain's Got Talent, The Wright Stuff, ITV News, QVC.*

Radio: Various radio phone-ins.

Her one-woman show – *War: You're a Whore and a Bore Says the Law!* – a musical about the negative factors of World War One, was widely praised.

Candy's theatre company, Shakespeare Not Stirred!, tours the good bits of Shakespeare's plays around old people's nursing homes. Candy also teaches, and loves nothing more than passing her experience and skills onto the young stars of tomorrow.

Candy is thrilled to be making her West End debut here performing in the National's new outdoor 'Random Red Shed' space, and would like to thank her parents for their continued and loving support. She would like to dedicate this performance to the memory of her grandma, Ethel, who inspired her to live her dream. And, of course, Nicky, her husband and director of this show – for giving her the chance to shine. And God. For giving her belief. And her best friend, Natasha, who has always been there for her. And not forgetting Flopsy – sadly missed, but never forgotten.

For further information on Candy you can follow her on Facebook, Twitter, SoundCloud, Instagram and YouTube. For fan club details: www.candyiscool.show.biz.

Actors – having a degree doesn't make you a better actor. And having your own album doesn't make you a better singer, dear.

The Actor's Timetable

An actor, just like an athlete, has to make sacrifices in order to perform and maintain their professional physique at all times. There will often be horrendous demands put upon the actor and their family – and this is a fact that simply has to be accepted. Any actor will at some point be asked to work irregular hours, and be forced to go out boozing until 4 a.m. in the morning – followed by an all-day lie-in. Some people find this very difficult, but it is an integral part of being an actor.

Of course, an actor's daily routine varies depending on whether they are rehearsing or performing. Rehearsals will generally take place during the day, and performances during the evening. Unless, of course, you are doing a Theatre in Education tour. In which case, good luck, dear.

Here are some examples of an actor's daily timetable (both that of a *dedicated* and *normal* actor). If you recognise the *normal* timetable, try following the *dedicated* one in your next show. You will be surprised at the results. And Doctor Theatre will be very proud of you, dear.

A *Dedicated* Actor's Daily Timetable When Rehearsing

6.00 – Wake up. Take a cold shower.

6.15 – Eat porridge and drink a big glass of water.

6.30 – Do a physical and vocal warm-up.

7.00 – Read through your script, and walk through the scenes.

8.00 – Travel to the rehearsal space. Write things in your Equity diary.

8.30 – Buy doughnuts for the company.

8.45 – Arrive at the rehearsal space. Put on a tight-fitting crop-top.

8.50 – Jump around pretending to be Darcey Bussell.

9.00 – Arrange your script around the floor and leap from one page to the next in chronological order.

9.30 – Rest and wait for the director to arrive – and when they do, ask lots of relevant questions.

10.00–13.00 – Rehearse.

13.00–14.00 – Lunch. Take out your prepared salad and water. Eat slowly whilst reading a copy of *The Stage*.

14.00–18.00 – Rehearse.

18.00 – Gym.

19.30 – Eat a healthy, balanced meal of vegetables, protein and carbohydrate. Drink green tea. Have the original cast recording of *Whistle Down the Wind* playing in the background.

20.00 – Re-read your script and think about your character.

21.00 – Find an empty space and meditate on a copy of Peter Brook's *The Empty Space*.

22.00 – Put a copy of the script under your pillow and sleep.

A *Normal* Actor's Daily Timetable When Rehearsing

9.40 – Roll out of bed.

9.45 – Buy coffee.

10.00–13.00 – Rehearse

13.00–14.00 – Pub.

14.00–18.00 – Rehearse.

18.00–22.00 – Pub.

23.00 – Go home.

23.30 – Check Facebook, Twitter and your favourite porn site.

00.59 – Script work.

1.00 – Bed.

A *Dedicated* Actor's Daily Timetable When Performing

11.00 – Wake up.

12.00 – Vocal and physical warm-up.

13.00 – Think about your performance from the night before and make notes.

14.00 – A light lunch of salad and tuna. Read one of Stanislavsky's books.

15.00 – Yoga.

16.30 – Visit your agent and tell them how grateful you are for their involvement in your life. Also remind them that you are available for voice-over work, adverts, and small film roles during your current show.

17.00 – Buy coffee, walk around the West End, and chat to other actors doing the same thing.

18.00 – Use a piano at the theatre to go through your repertoire.

18.25 – Company warm-up.

19.30 – Perform show.

22.00 – Head home.

23.00 – Think about your performance, and how you can improve it tomorrow.

23.30 – Call your agent and wish them goodnight.

00.00 – Go through some acting speeches in front of your partner, flatmates, or mum and dad. Ask for constructive feedback.

1.00 – A quick prayer to Doctor Theatre. Bed.

A *Normal* Actor's Daily Timetable When Performing

13.00 – Wake up.

14.00–17.00 – Watch DVD boxset.

18.00 – Head to theatre, buying a coffee en route.

18.30 – Company warm-up.

19.30 – Perform show.

22.00 – Pub.

00.00 – Club.

4.00 – Bed.

A *Theatre in Education* Actor's Daily Timetable

3.00 – Wake up and drive minivan to the first school.

4.30 – Arrive at school.

4.45 – Drink strong coffee.

5.00 – Start unloading your set from the van.

5.30 – Drink Red Bull.

6.00 – Meet the caretaker and become acquainted with the school hall.

6.15 – Start putting your set up.

7.00 – Drink Red Bull.

7.30 – Finish putting up the set and sort out your costumes.

7.45 – Consume a bacon, egg and sausage sandwich.

8.00 – Introduce yourself to all the teachers.

8.30 – Drink Red Bull.

8.45 – Have a quick runthrough of the show.

9.00 – Perform the show to a hall crammed full of Haribo-sponsored kids.

10.00 – Finish performance and clean the floor of children's wee, vomit and tears.

10.30 – Force the teachers to go back to work.

11.15 – Take down set and pack into van.

11.30 – Drink Red Bull.

12.00 – Drive to second school and repeat above steps.

18.00 – Drive to budget hostel, drink copious amounts of alcohol, and sleep with each other.

A *TV* Actor's Timetable

It is not worth including a timetable for TV actors because their schedule is: arrive on set, go into trailer, sleep in trailer, do a scene, sleep in trailer, wait in trailer, eat in trailer, moan in trailer, go home.

Actors – writing, directing, producing and acting in your own show does not make you talented. It makes you schizophrenic, dear.

THE
CURTAIN CALL

OR
'GOOD GOD, IS THAT THE TIME? WE'RE GOING TO MISS THE TRAIN HOME.'

A career in theatre does not guarantee wealth or fame. It just guarantees a career of joy, passion, and fun in the dark, dear.

How to Know When You've 'Made It'

Throughout your career there will be moments when you feel successful and moments when you feel like a worthless nobody. It is inevitable. And is to be expected in a business that is constantly changing. No actor is permanently in work and, indeed, an actor who is deemed famous one year may be forgotten about by the next. It can be harsh, brutal, and downright annoying.

The joy of the business is that at any time your life could change in an instant. You could one day find yourself waltzing into an audition, impressing the panel, and being offered the job of Superman in the forthcoming remake of the remake. And then you are set! Suddenly you are working, you are earning big bucks, and all of your ex-lovers regret dumping you. It is a magnificent feeling. And one which can make years of hardship seem worthwhile.

However, it is vital that you have actually 'made it' before you start behaving like a star and spending all your money in The Ivy, The Groucho and Pizza Express. If you are unsure, here are some telltale signs:

- You are allowed into the theatre after the half-hour call.
- Your name is on all the publicity material.
- You are asked to do radio and television interviews.

- The musical director is happy to change the key of a song for you.

- It is not expected that you will attend the company warm-up.

- You get dressing room number 1.

- Members of the ensemble laugh at all of your jokes.

- You will be able to sleep with any of the front-of-house team.

- You can give notes to the rest of the company.

- The company manager is nice to you.

- You will never be expected to sing harmony lines.

- The producer will know your name.

....

The AA called. They're starting a new kind of insurance – Actors' Advance. It protects me if I employ a bad one, dear.

....

Surviving

It is hard enough trying to survive in any business in the present climate – but surviving as an actor is harder still. It is one of the most competitive jobs in the world, and everyone wants to get to the top. The business is constantly changing – and to survive in it, you must too. I'd like to offer some simple, yet rather effective survival tips.

Survival Tips

- Never try and be too different. Whilst I'm sure you were told at drama school to make sure you 'stand out', you should always make sure you don't stand out *too much*. There is nothing worse than an actor being different just for the sake of being different. You *are* different. You are you. And that is enough. Just deliver the song, the script, the dance or the striptease to the best of your ability – and you will stand out. For the right reasons, for being good.

- Be careful who you get drunk with. There's no point making a complete ass of yourself in front of the most important casting director in London. Unless they are buying you lots of drinks – in which case you should go for it. But always be on your guard. Don't talk about your acting roles too much, and never break into a drunken chorus of 'Stars'. Chances are you won't do yourself, or the song, any justice. Unless you are Russell Crowe. Then it doesn't really matter.

- It is your career, so control it. There's no point auditioning to be a costume character at Disneyland if you actually want to work for the RSC (unless, of course, you want to sleep with Minnie Mouse). Plan your career, and imagine what kind of CV you want to have. Only do those jobs that you have a genuine desire to do. Don't do them just because your agent wants you to. It is *your* career. You decided to be an actor – so now decide what kind of an actor you are.

- Be prepared for those times when you are not acting. This is the hardest part of being an actor. You can feel miserable, unwanted, ugly – and poor! But don't be disheartened, every actor goes through it – it is part of an actor's life. So be ready for it, plan for it. Everyone has to pay their bills, and still have enough money to get sloshed at the weekend, so be aware that you will invariably end up doing some silly jobs at some point. And why not? Do it! Do those silly temp jobs, because you never know who you will meet. That person handing out flyers could be the next artistic director of the National Theatre. Or it could even be the current artistic director.

- But what to do when you are feeling down? Well, I suggest this: do a lunge, or a ball-change, or simply display your jazz hands for the world to see. It's amazing what a spontaneous jazz hand can do to lift your mood. And indeed not only *your* mood, but the mood of everyone else around you. And a ball-change? A ball-change is accepted anywhere. Do it in your gym, your local Wetherspoon's, and even The Ivy (although I would suggest not doing it in your local public toilets unless you are George Michael). This simple formula is a sure way to raise your spirits in moments of negativity.

You are a performer. But you are also a person. And everyone finds it hard sometimes. And I, for one, admire each and every one of you. So keep striving, keep learning, and keep smiling, dear.

Actors – if you are struggling, an easy way to success is by changing your surname to Strallen, dear.

The Future

Theatre is currently in a very good place. The West End is flourishing and touring shows are doing exceptional business. It really is remarkable. My only concern is the ridiculous increase in ticket prices.

It's perfectly clear why this happens. Making theatre is risky. And making theatre that actually makes a profit is rare. This is a big misconception about theatre. Producers aren't all millionaires, sadly. It is a difficult business. What works one year will not work the next. Even transferring a hit show from Broadway doesn't necessarily mean it will be a hit in the West End – and vice versa. It is a hard business – and even before a show actually makes it to the stage, sometimes it is best to pull out, even if this means losing thousands of pounds.

The problem is that the cost of putting on theatre gets more expensive every year, and a very obvious way to help with this is by upping ticket prices – because someone will always be prepared to pay the premium price (unless the show is a flop – in which case no one will!). The worry is that this trend is making theatre, once again, something of an elitist activity. There are only a certain number of people that can afford to pay £60 a ticket – indeed, the average family of four would find it an impossibility. And this is not fair. To make relevant theatre for a current audience we need to make it accessible to everyone. Many people simply are not prepared to take the gamble of paying such enormous amounts of money to go and see a show, particularly when they have no guarantee that they will enjoy it.

Whilst I am well aware that some theatres offer cheaper seats – and you can purchase tickets for around £15 in the upper circle – these seats invariably are not that good. I am a big fan of places like Shakespeare's Globe where £5 standing tickets are available, and theatres that offer £25 day seats – but not everyone is able or willing to stand outside in the bitter cold to get a couple of tickets, which even then are not guaranteed. There are also websites that offer reduced-rate tickets, but to find these deals can become something of a challenge. Of course, it is wonderful that people are prepared to go to such lengths to see a show – indeed, it only shows the increasing demand for high-quality theatre – but these tickets should be easier and more frequently available.

We simply all need to start working together a bit more. All of us producers, all theatres and companies, particularly in the West End, should be trying to help attract new audiences, and work on getting ticket prices back down. Only when we are all fighting the same cause will this begin to happen.

And we need to be braver. We need to push forward and find the new artists, composers, and creators of tomorrow. The trend to employ reality TV stars or movie actors solely to get bums on seats is understandable – but until this current fad is ended then it will continue to gather speed. Look at some of our bravest and most modern theatre companies – Paines Plough, Kneehigh, Frantic Assembly, Punchdrunk – who, through the quality and strength of their work, have forged a faithful and exciting audience of their own. Their work is attracting a whole new and different theatre audience, which is thrilling. And with projects like NT Live – where theatre productions are broadcast live in cinemas – theatre is becoming accessible to anyone and everyone wherever they are. But, of course, the true thrill of theatre is seeing it live, being in a building with hundreds of others, all gathering to witness an event, a celebration, something which has been created to be viewed in a specific space, by a collective audience who are there for that purpose. And that is the joy of theatre.

Whilst TV is changing, and the internet is an extension of our everyday life experience, theatre has something unique to offer. It is not recorded, it is not on a screen in front of us, we cannot pause it whilst we take a phone call, or quickly scan over it and press the refresh button. It is something that demands our focus, our energy and participation – and with that come the rewards of being involved in a live event. And luckily for us all, this makes it an art form that will never die. It is something that has the power to move, to affect, to challenge, and constantly to reflect humanity. And that is why I adore it.

Anyhow, I think I've kept you long enough now. Thank you for your time and patience. I must be off. My Jean Valjean teddy is waiting with a nice chilled bottle of Dom.

It's been emotional. Wrap up warm, drive carefully, and have a safe journey home.

Bless you.

Kindest,

WEP

x

Nighty night. Don't let the jazz hands bite, dear.

WEST END LEADING ROLE VOUCHER

This voucher entitles the bearer to play the lead in any West End musical for one performance only. Simply present this voucher to a member of the front-of-house team and inform them you will be playing the leading role.

Name:

Vocal range:

Inside leg (inches):

Show:

Date:

Terms and Conditions: This voucher allows the above named person to play the leading role of their choice *outside* their chosen theatre. It does not allow them on stage, backstage, front of house, or inside the director's bedroom.

'TOUCH AN ACTOR' VOUCHER

This voucher entitles the bearer to one free touch in West End Producer's 'Touch an Actor' Scheme. Simply present this voucher to your chosen actor and you are allowed to touch them for a duration of no longer than ten seconds.

Your name:

Name of actor:

Date:

Area for touching:

Duration of touch (ten seconds max):

Terms and Conditions: This voucher will be redeemable only once West End Producer's 'Touch an Actor' Scheme is operational. It allows the above named person to touch their chosen actor for up to ten seconds. Areas not accessible by this voucher: groin region, bra region, bottom region, any injury. If you ask nicely some actors will allow you to briefly tickle their balls.

BLANK PAGE FOR NOTES FROM THE RESIDENT DIRECTOR (To be ignored later on)

BLANK PAGE TO WRITE YOUR LINES WHEN IN ACTORS' DETENTION

**BLANK PAGE TO DRAW PICTURES OF ANDREW
LLOYD WEBBER AND CAMERON MACKINTOSH***

* Please tweet your drawings to me (@westendproducer)

**BLANK PAGE FOR PRACTISING YOUR
STAGE KISSING**

**BLANK PAGE FOR DOODLES WHEN YOU'RE BORED
IN A NOTES SESSION**

**BLANK PAGE TO RIP OUT, SCRUNCH UP, AND
THROW AT BAD ACTORS (Bactors)**

**BLANK PAGE TO KEEP A TALLY OF HOW MANY
AUDITIONS YOU HAVE IN A YEAR
(Less than 10 is worrying, but more than 100 is
showing off, dear)**

**BLANK PAGE FOR WRITING RUDE THINGS ABOUT
ACTORS YOU ARE UNDERSTUDYING**
(This can be very therapeutic, dear)